P

PEOPLE AND ORGANISATIONS

Managing Activities

MICHAEL ARMSTRONG

INSTITUTE OF PERSONNEL AND DEVELOPMENT

Design by Curve

Typeset by Fakenham Photosetting Ltd, Fakenham, Norfolk

Printed in Great Britain by
the Cromwell Press, Trowbridge, Wiltshire

British Library Cataloguing in Publication Data
A catalogue record of this book is available from the British Library

ISBN 0-85292-781-9

INSTITUTE OF PERSONNEL
AND DEVELOPMENT

IPD House, Camp Road, London SW19 4UX
Tel: 0181 971 9000   Fax: 0181 263 3333
Registered office as above. Registered Charity No. 1038333
A company limited by guarantee. Registered in England No. 2931892

Contents

Foreword

Welcome to this series of texts designed to complement the Core Management syllabus. The role of the personnel and development practitioner has become an important part of the total management of all types of organisation in the private, public and voluntary sectors. A fundamental element of that role is the ability to comprehend and contribute to the overall goals, performance and outcomes of organisations. This is the purpose of the Core Management syllabus: to equip personnel and development practitioners to understand and appreciate complex business and managerial issues and to develop their skills so that they can play a full role in that process.

Michael Armstrong's book examines the nature of managing business organisations. Whatever the specific sector, product or service, there are certain key generic activities that affect all managers. Michael Armstrong demonstrates that operating as an effective manager requires a clear appreciation of the nature of managerial work, its location in the structure, functions and power relationships within organisations, and an ability to comprehend and operate in the context of change, improvement and customer care.

Professor Ian J Beardwell
Head, Department of HRM
Leicester Business School
De Montfort University
Leicester

Introduction

WHAT THIS BOOK IS ABOUT

This book is about the management of work within the context of the organisation. It is concerned with the activities carried out in organisations to achieve their aims and meet the expectations and needs of their stakeholders – owners, managers, employees, customers, suppliers and the public at large. It addresses the contextual factors within organisations which affect how they go about their business. These include the culture of the organisation, the type and range of activities carried out, the processes of authority and control used within the organisation, and the implications of the use of power and the existence of political forces and tensions. The book looks at what managers do when they plan, organise, co-ordinate, control, direct, implement, monitor and evaluate the activities for which they are responsible. It recognises, however, that the nature of managerial work can be fragmented, varied and characterised by brief bursts of activity.

Throughout the book the term 'manager' is used to denote anyone who gets things done with and through other people. It therefore covers such roles and job titles as those of team leader and supervisor. The term 'business' is used to cover any organisation, whether it is in the private sector and concerned with making profits (as well, it is to be hoped, as other things), or in the public or voluntary sectors and concerned with the efficient and effective delivery of services. But organisations in the public and voluntary sectors have got to be just as *businesslike* as those in the private sector. To refer to them as 'businesses' recognises this fact.

THE AIM OF THE BOOK

The aim has been to provide a general introduction into all aspects of managing a business and the activities carried out within a business. The book is structured round the core management professional standards developed by the Institute of Personnel and Development (IPD) for 'Managing Activities'. These in turn were influenced by the NVQ definitions of standards for their managerial modules, especially those defined for Level 4.

The book is therefore inspired by the following rationale produced by the IPD for the Managing Activities module.

> Managerial work is complex and fragmented in its nature. The very term implies a range of behaviour from administration to inspirational leadership, and job descriptions for managers may differ in the extreme. This module examines the various ways in which activities are managed within the workplace, including techniques, relationships and demands. The ability of the manager to communicate effectively is, of course, crucial and will be demonstrated through the learning outcomes which require a variety of approaches.
>
> All of this takes place within the cultural and structural framework of the organisation in the current context of change for continuous improvement. As competition increases and resources become scarce, there is significant benefit to be gained from the understanding of how activities can and should be managed, including techniques, relationships and demands.

MANAGEMENT STANDARDS

The book also takes account of the management standards produced by the Management Charter Institute (MCI).

The standards as presented for 'key role A', *Manage Activities*, state that they describe 'the manager's work in managing the operation to meet customers' requirements and continuously improve its performance'. The units relating to this key role are:

1 Maintain activities to meet requirements.

2 Manage activities to meet requirements.

3 Manage activities to meet customer requirements.

4 Contribute to improvements at work.

5 Manage change in organisational activities.

6 Review external and internal operating environments.

7 Establish strategies to guide the work of the organisation.

8 Evaluate and improve organisational performance.

PLAN OF THE BOOK

The book is divided into three sections as set out in the Indicative Content of the Managing Activities module:

1 The nature of managerial work

2 The work environment

3 Quality and continuous improvement.

Part 1

THE NATURE OF MANAGERIAL WORK

1   What managers do – fragmentation, variety and brevity

This chapter is concerned with what managers do. The traditional model of management is that it is a logical and systematic process of planning, organising, motivating and controlling. But the work that managers actually carry out is characterised by fragmentation, variety and brevity. They may indeed be engaged in planning, organising, directing and controlling activities from time to time. However, because of the pressures under which they work and the constant need to cope with new situations, their working life is much less orderly than the classic management theories indicate.

On completing the chapter, a reader will:

- know what a manager is and what management is about

- be familiar with the classic theories of management which emphasise order, structure and control

- be aware of more recent attempts to describe what managers do, based on empirical studies which indicate that – rather than being ordered, structured and controlled – management tends to be fragmented, varied and governed to a large degree by events over which managers have little or no control

- appreciate the competencies managers need to possess to carry out their roles.

DEFINITION OF MANAGEMENT

A manager can be defined as 'someone who is responsible for the operation of a discrete organisational unit or function and who has been given authority over those working in that unit or function'.

The key words in this definition are *responsibility* and *authority*. Responsibility involves people being accountable for what they do or cause others to do. Authority means having the right or power to get people to do things. It involves the exercise of personal influence arising from position or knowledge.

The definition also indicates that a manager is someone who leads a team of people. This is the usual meaning attached to the term 'manager' and is the one adopted in this book. But people can be called managers even if they have no staff – for example, an investment manager could be solely responsible for controlling investments without any help. And managers are, of course, also responsible for managing other resources: finance, facilities, information, time, and themselves.

People can be specialists or professionals as well as managers, and much of their time could be spent in using their professional expertise to make decisions and solve problems rather than in getting someone else to do that for them.

Managers are like everyone else in an organisation in that they carry out roles. A role is the part a person plays in fulfilling his or her responsibilities. A role is not the same as a job, as set out in a job description, which is a list of duties and, perhaps, a statement of the overall purpose of the job. The role someone plays relates to how the person carries out the job. It is the concept and performance of a role that distinguishes individuals in organisational positions through the way they confront the demands and situational pressures within the role.

The demands of a role can be classified in terms of explicitness, clarity and coherence. They can refer to expectations – what *must* be done, what *should* be done and what *can* be done. 'Role expectations' consist of what individuals perceive to be their positions and the demands attached to them. People interpret what they are expected to do in the light of their perceptions of the context in which they work. When confronted with new demands or pressures from outside the organisation or from people within the organisation, they may have to re-interpret their roles and be prepared to respond flexibly. Roles, especially managerial roles, can therefore be fluid, and managers have to adapt rapidly – they cannot remain within the rigid confines of a prescribed set of duties. 'Role performance' refers to managers' actual behaviour, either in response to perceived expectations or in pursuing individual aims and projects. Managers may have to work in conditions of role ambiguity, when they are not sure what they are expected to do, or role conflict, when what they feel they should do is not in accord with what others believe they should do.

In carrying out their roles people are engaged in activities and tasks. Activities comprise what managers do – their behaviour. Tasks are what managers are expected or seek to achieve. In defining managerial work a distinction has been made by Hales[1] between managers' behaviours and actions and the desired outcomes of those behaviours. This can be described as an 'input-process-output' model in which inputs are the knowledge and skills managers bring to their role, process is their behaviour in using their knowledge and skills to make decisions and take action, and output is the result or outcome of the behaviour.

The process of management can crudely be defined as getting things done through people. But there is more to it than that. Management can be described as deciding what to do and *then* getting it done through people. But even that description is insufficient. Managers work *with* people (their colleagues, customers, outside suppliers and their teams) as well as *through* people. Managers are part of the action. They are not there simply to tell other people what to do. In one sense, the members of their teams are their internal customers to whom managers have the obligation to provide help and support, as well as to provide direction so as to ensure that the required end results are achieved.

Managers are also concerned with other resources besides

those working directly for them. Managers have to manage themselves and make the best use of their key resources – expertise, leadership qualities and, importantly, time. They may have to 'manage' or at least interact with other people on inter-functional teams as well as with colleagues who are their internal customers. Managers are also managed, and they may – more or less subtly – have to manage their bosses to ensure that the right direction, guidance and support are provided. Finally, managers have to manage other resources: money, equipment, plant and facilities. They may do this through other people, but they could, for example, be entirely responsible for financial management. To emphasise this multifaceted role, a better definition of management might be:

• deciding what to do and getting it done through and with other people by making the best use of the available resources.

So far, so good – but this definition contains a degree of precision which may not exist in practice. Management could be defined much more broadly, albeit tautologically, as what managers do. Silverman and Jones[2] have suggested that managers actively define their own work and create its constituent activities – communication is not simply what managers take a long time doing but the medium through which managerial work is constituted. As Hales[3] points out, 'The work of managers is the management of their work,' or as Gowler and Legge[4] contend, 'The meaning of management is the management of meaning.'

It is against this somewhat nebulous background that the classic theories of management and the later finding of the empiricists should be considered. These are examined below.

THE CLASSIC CONCEPTS OF MANAGEMENT

The classic writers on management set out to define the nature of managerial work in terms of basic universal elements. These were believed to provide a framework for the analysis and conduct of the managerial task.

Henri Fayol

The classic framework was developed in1912 by a pioneer writer on management, Henri Fayol[5], who based it on an analysis of his experience as a practising manager. He stated that 'All undertakings require planning, organising, command, co-ordination and control to function properly.'

Luther Gullick

A later (1937) theorist of the classic school was Luther Gullick[6], who expanded Fayol's concept into the acronym POSDCORB, which stands for:

- *Planning* – working out in broad outline the things that need to be done and the methods for doing them to accomplish the purpose set for the enterprise

- *Organising* – establishing the formal structure of an organisation through which work subdivisions are arranged, defined and co-ordinated for the whole enterprise

- *Staffing* – bringing in and training the staff and maintaining favourable conditions of work – the personnel function

- *Directing* – making decisions and continuously embodying them in specific general orders and instruction, and serving as the leader of the enterprise

- *Co-ordinating* – interrelating the various parts of the work – an all-important duty

- *Reporting* – keeping those to whom executives are responsible informed as to what is going on, which includes keeping oneself and one's subordinates informed through records, research and inspection

- *Budgeting* – financial planning, accounting and control.

The contemporary version of classic theory

The contemporary and widely recognised version of these lists divides managerial work into four main elements:

- *Planning* – deciding on a course of action to achieve a

desired result and focusing attention on objectives and standards and the programmes required to achieve them

- *Organising* – setting up and staffing the most appropriate organisation to achieve the aim

- *Motivating* – exercising leadership to motivate people to work together smoothly and to the best of their ability as part of a team

- *Controlling* – measuring and monitoring the progress of work in relation to the plan and taking corrective action when required.

These headings have become the common parlance of management, but their usefulness and universality have been challenged.

Challenges to the classic school

Sune Carlsson[7], a researcher into management, wrote that:

> If we ask a managing director when he is co-ordinating, or how much co-ordination he has been doing during the day, he would not know, and even the most highly skilled observer would not know either. The same holds true of the concepts of planning, command, organisation and control.

And Rosemary Stewart[8] pointed out that:

> They [management theorists] could talk about *the* manager's job because their description of his functions was so general as to be universally valid; but such a level of generalisation has a very limited usefulness in practice.

Common sense as well as the evidence collected by the empirical researchers as described below tell us that managers do not sit down and divide their day into neat segments labelled 'planning', 'organising', 'motivating' and 'controlling'.

But the classic concept of management should not be dismissed out of hand. Planning, organising, motivating and controlling are what managers do at least some of the time, even if each takes place haphazardly, almost unconsciously, during a complex working day. And it is clear that when the originator of this school, Henri Fayol, writes: 'In every case the organisation has to carry out [the following] managerial duties', he is making it clear that he is writing about management in general, not the behaviour of individual managers. In fact, the classic theorists tried to describe what *management* is. They did not attempt to describe how individual managers behave. That was left to the empiricists who succeeded them.

> Think about any manager you know well, or, if appropriate, your own work as a manager. To what extent can you identify specific planning, organising, motivating and controlling activities? Give examples.

Sune Carlsson

Sune Carlsson[9] studied the work of nine Swedish managing directors, and his findings can be summarised under three headings:

- *Working time* – Executives were alone for not more than one hour a day but the typical 'alone' intervals were only of 10–15 minutes' duration. The MDs spent their days being constantly interrupted and they had remarkably little control over how they spent their time.

- *Communication patterns* – Chief executives initiate far fewer letters a day than they receive. The average time spent with visitors was three-and-a-half hours a day.

- *Work content* – One of the main activities of the chief executives was to keep themselves informed.

Rosemary Stewart

Rosemary Stewart[10] studied 160 senior and middle managers for four weeks each. Her main findings on how they spent their time were:

- The managers worked an average of 42 hours per week.

- Discussions took 60 per cent of their time: 43 per cent informal, 7 per cent committee, 6 per cent telephoning and 4 per cent social activity.

- They spent 34 per cent of their time alone, 25 per cent with their immediate subordinates, 8 per cent with their superiors, 25 per cent with colleagues and 5 per cent with external contacts.

- Fragmentation in work was considerable. In the four-week period, managers averaged only nine periods of 30 minutes or more without interruption, and averaged 20 contacts a day, 12 of them fleeting ones (of less than five minutes' duration).

Henry Mintzberg

Henry Mintzberg[11] observed five chief executives over a period of five weeks. He found that the proportion of time they spent on different activities was:

	Average	Range
	%	%
Desk work	22	16–38
Telephone calls	6	4–9
Scheduled meetings	59	38–75
Unscheduled meetings	10	3–8
Tours	3	0–10
Proportion of activities lasting less than nine minutes	49	40–56
Proportion of activities lasting longer than 60 minutes	10	5–13

The managers' days were characterised by a large number of brief informal two-person contacts (telephone calls and unscheduled meetings) and relatively few scheduled meetings which nevertheless took most of their time. Subordinates consumed about half the managers' contact time and were involved in two-thirds of the contacts. The managers initiated less than one-third of their contacts and only 5 per cent were scheduled regularly.

The broad conclusions emerging from this study confirmed that 'management' is

- highly interactive

- very much concerned with communication

- about getting things done with or through other people

- not much about office work.

Mintzberg also contrasted findings such as these on the work of managers with those of the classic school, stating that his own results 'paint an interesting picture, one as different from Fayol's view as a cubist abstract is from a Renaissance painting'.

Leonard Sayles

Leonard Sayles[12] interviewed 75 lower- and middle-level managers in a large American corporation. He identified three aspects of managerial work in his analysis.

- *Managers as participants in external work flows* – which leads to seven basic relationships with people outside their immediate managerial responsibility
  - trading relationships: making arrangements with other members of the organisation to get work done
  - work-flow relationships: making contacts concerning the work preceding or following that supervised by the manager
  - service relationships: making contacts relating to the giving or receiving of services or support by specialist groups – for example, market research or maintenance
  - advisory relationships: arranging the provision of counsel and advice to line managers by experts – for example, in industrial relations
  - auditing relationships: making contacts with those who evaluate or appraise organisational work – for example, personnel in management accounts or quality control

- stabilisation relationships: making contacts with those who are empowered to limit or control the manager's decision in accordance with organisational policy – for example, concerning production planning and control
- innovative relationships: making contacts with groups specially isolated to perform a research function.
- *Managers as leaders* – which results in three basic types of leadership behaviour
  - leadership as direction: getting subordinates to respond to the requests of the manager
  - leadership as response: responding to initiatives from subordinates who are seeking aid or support
  - leadership as representation: representing subordinates in contact with other parts of the organisation.
- *Managers as monitors* – in which managers follow the progress of work through the system, detect variations and initiate action as required.

Peter Lawrence

Peter Lawrence[13] observed the work of 16 German and 25 British general and production managers. His analysis of the proportion of time spent on different activities was:

	German %	British %
Formal scheduled recurrent meetings	9.78	15.50
Convened special-purpose meetings	12.62	14.46
Ad-hoc discussions	20.07	17.93
Time spent in works	16.87	17.35
Telephoning	10.56	7.23
Office work	11.56	11.16
Explanations to researcher	10.45	13.08
Miscellaneous	8.02	4.08

Note that in both Germany and Britain the highest proportion of time was spent in ad-hoc discussions. This demonstrates the extent to which managerial work is unplanned and frequently involves brief responses to sudden events.

THE FRAGMENTARY NATURE OF MANAGERIAL WORK

The research into how managers spend their time confirms that their activities are characterised by fragmentation, brevity and variety. Because of the open-ended nature of their work, managers feel compelled to perform a great variety of tasks at an unrelenting pace. As Mintzberg[14] comments:

> The manager actually appears to prefer brevity and interruption to his [sic] work. He becomes conditioned by his workload; he develops an appreciation of the opportunity cost of his own time; and he lives continuously with an awareness of what else might or must be done at any time. Superficiality is an occupational hazard of a manager's job ... The manager gravitates to the more active elements of his work – the current, the specific, the well-defined, the non-routine activities.

He also indicated that even senior managers spend little time on planning, are subject to constant interruption, hold short face-to-face meetings which flit from topic to topic, and respond to the initiatives of others far more than they initiate themselves.

> From your observation of managers at work, how realistic do you think Mintzberg's analysis is? Can anything be done to change this situation?

Why does this happen?

Fragmentation, variety and brevity in managerial work occur for the following six reasons.

1 Managers are largely concerned with dealing with people – their staff and their internal and external customers. But people's behaviour is often unpredictable; their demands and responses are conditioned by the constantly changing circumstances in which they exist, by the pressures to which *they* have to respond, and by their individual wants and needs. Conflicts arise and have to be dealt with on the spot.

2 Managers are not always in a position to control the events that affect their work. Sudden demands are imposed upon them by other people within the organisation or from outside. Crises can occur which they are unable to predict.

3 Managers are expected to be decisive and deal with situations as they crop up. Their best-laid plans are therefore often disrupted; their established priorities have to be abandoned.

4 Managers are at the beck and call of their superiors who also have to respond instantly to new demands and crises.

5 Managers often work in conditions of turbulence and ambiguity. They are not clear about what is expected of them when new situations arise. They therefore tend to be reactive rather than proactive, dealing with immediate problems rather than trying to anticipate them.

6 For all the reasons given above, managers are subject to constant interruptions. They have little chance to settle down and think about their plans and priorities or to spend enough time in studying control information (see Chapter 2, page 43) to assist in maintaining a 'steady state' as far as their own activities go.

WHAT MANAGERS ACTUALLY DO

What managers do is dependent on their function, level, organisation (the type, structure, culture, size) and their working environment generally (the extent to which it is turbulent/predictable/pressurised/steady). Individual managers adapt to these circumstances in different ways and operate more or less successfully in accordance with their own perceptions of the behaviour expected of them, their experience of what has or has not worked in the past, and their own personal characteristics.

There are, however, some typical characteristics of managerial work, which are:

• reaction and non-reflection

- identifying and making choices

- communication

- identifying tasks

- the varying nature of the work.

Reaction and non-reflection

As Hales[15] suggests, much of what managers do is, of necessity, an unreflecting response to circumstances. Managers are usually not so much slow and methodical decision-makers as doers who have to react rapidly to problems as they arise and think on their feet. Much time is spent in day-to-day troubleshooting.

Identifying and making choices

Stewart[16] established that managers exercise choice about their work. They informally negotiate widely different interpretations of the boundaries and dimensions of ostensibly identical jobs, with particular emphasis upon the development of 'personal domain' (ie establishing their own territory and the rules that apply within it). Stewart[17] has also identified the choices which operate within the demands and constraints of managerial work. She suggests that the choices common to all managerial jobs are concerned with *content* (aspects of a job a manager chooses to emphasise, selections between aspects, and choices about risk-taking) and *methods* (how work is done).

Communication

Much managerial activity consists of asking or persuading others to do things which involves managers in face-to-face verbal communication of limited duration. Communication is not simply what managers spend a great deal of time doing but the medium through which managerial work is constituted.

Identifying tasks

Silverman and Jones[18] suggest that the typical work of a junior manager is the 'organisational work' of drawing upon an evolving stock of knowledge about 'normal' procedures and routines in order to identify and negotiate the accomplishment of problems and tasks.

The varying nature of the work

As Hales[19] points out, the character of work varies by duration, timespan, recurrence, unexpectedness and source. Little time is spent on any one activity and in particular on the conscious, systematic formulation of plans. Planning and decision-making tend to take place in the course of other activities. Managerial activities are riven by contradictions, cross-pressures, and the need to cope with and reconcile conflict. A lot of time is spent by managers accounting for and explaining what they do, in informal relationships and in 'participating'.

WHAT MANAGERS CAN DO ABOUT IT

To a degree, managers have simply to put up with the circumstances in which they work, as described above: they have to manage in conditions of turbulence, uncertainty and ambiguity. That is why one of the characteristics of effective managers is their resilience – they have to be able to cope with these inevitable pressures. But there are competencies (as described below) and skills (as discussed in the next chapter) which can help them to manage in these circumstances. To a considerable extent it is up to managers to be aware of these requirements, the behaviours expected of them, and the skills they can use to help in carrying out their often demanding responsibilities. They must treat these as guidelines for personal development plans. Managers can learn from the example of their bosses, by guidance from those bosses and from mentors, and through formal training courses – but self-managed learning is all-important.

MANAGERIAL EFFECTIVENESS

Managerial effectiveness 'denotes the extent to which what managers *actually* do matches what they are *supposed* to do'.[20] It is about performance, which refers both to what people do (their achievements) and how people do it (their behaviour). To measure effectiveness, it is necessary to understand and define both sides of the equation – that is, inputs (skills and behaviour) and outputs (results). The measurement of effectiveness and performance therefore compares expectations about achievements and behaviour with actual results and behaviour.

When assessing managerial effectiveness in terms of behaviour the concept of the competent manager as originally developed by Boyatzis[21] is relevant. Boyatzis defines competence as 'A capacity that exists in a person that leads to behaviour that meets the job demands within the parameters of the organisational environment, and that in turn brings about desired results.'

Later commentators distinguished between *competences* and *competencies*.

Competences
Competences are the things people need to be able to understand and do to perform effectively. They provide the basis for national vocational qualifications and professional standards such as those produced by the Institute of Personnel and Development and the Management Charter Institute.

Competencies
Competencies are the sort of behaviours that produce effective performance. They are defined in the competency frameworks and profiles many organisations are now using to provide guidance on selection, on training and development, and sometimes on increases in pay. A competency framework or profile provides guidance to managers on the sort of behaviour expected of them. Such frameworks can be used to provide criteria for assessing performance in its widest sense.

Competency magazine in 1996 reported that the 10 most common behaviours sought by the 126 organisations they surveyed were:

• communication

- achievement-results-orientation
- customer focus
- teamwork
- leadership
- planning and organising
- commercial/business awareness
- flexibility/adaptability
- developing others
- problem-solving.

The MCI list of personal competencies

The Management Charter Institute has produced the following list of personal competencies which provide a useful guide to areas for personal development.

- building teams
    - Keep others informed about plans and progress.
    - Clearly identify what is required of others.
    - Invite others to contribute to planning and organising work.
- communicating
    - Identify the information needs of listeners.
    - Adopt communication styles appropriate to listeners and situations, including selection of an appropriate time and place.
    - Use a variety of media and communication aids to reinforce points and maintain interest.
- focusing on results
    - Maintain a focus on objectives.
    - Tackle problems and take advantage of opportunities as they arise.
    - Actively seek to do things better.
    - Use change as an opportunity for improvement.
    - Monitor quality of work and progress against plans.
- thinking and taking decisions

— Break processes down into tasks and activities.

— Identify a range of elements in and perspectives on a situation.

— Identify implications, consequences or causal relationships in a situation.

— Take decisions which are realistic for the situation.

> To what extent do you think it possible for managers themselves to develop their own competencies as set out above? How might they set about doing it? What help might they need?

SUMMARY

• A manager is someone who is responsible for the operation of a discrete organisational unit or function and who has been given authority over those working in that unit or function.

• Management is about deciding what to do and then getting it done through and with other people by making the best use of available resources.

• The classic writers defined the nature of management in terms of basic universal elements, eg planning, organising, directing and controlling.

• This does not, however, describe how managers actually spend their time which, as research has shown, is characterised by fragmentation, variety and brevity.

• Managers tend to be doers who react to events and think on their feet. They often exercise choice about what they do and how they do it. Much of the time of managers is spent in communicating. Planning tends to take place during the course of carrying out other activities.

• To cope with the nature of their work managers have to be resilient, but there are competencies and skills they can develop which will help them to perform effectively.

REFERENCES

1 HALES C. P. (1986) 'What managers do: a critical review of the evidence'. *Journal of Management Studies*. Vol. 23, No. 1, January, pp. 88–115.

2 SILVERMAN D. *and* JONES J. (1976) *Organisational Work*. London, Macmillan.

3 HALES, see Note 1 above.

4 GOWLER D. *and* LEGGE K. 'The meaning of management and the management of meaning: a view from social anthropology', in EARLE M.J. (ed) *Perspectives on Management: a Multidisciplinary Approach*. London, Oxford University Press, 1983.

5 FAYOL H. *General and Industrial Administration*. London, Pitman, 1949.

6 GULLICK L. 'Notes on the theory of organisations', in. GULLICK L. and URWICK L. (eds) *Papers on the Science of Administration*. New York, Columbia University Press, 1937.

7 CARLSSON S. *Executive Behaviour: A study of the workload and the working methods of managing directors*. Strömberg, 1951.

8 STEWART R. *Managers and their Jobs*. London, Macmillan, 1967.

9 CARLSSON, see Note 7 above.

10 STEWART, see Note 8 above.

11 MINTZBERG H. *The Nature of Managerial Work*. New York, Harper & Row, 1973.

12 SAYLES L.(1964) *Managerial Behaviour*. New York, McGraw-Hill, 1964.

13 LAWRENCE P. *Management in Action. London,* Routledge and Kegan Paul, 1984

14 MINTZBERG, see Note 11 above.

15 HALES, see Note 1 above.

16 STEWART R., SMITH P., BLAKE J. *and* WINGATE P. *The District Administrator in the National Health Service*. London, Pitman, 1980.

17 STEWART, see Note 8 above.

18 SILVERMAN *and* JONES, see Note 2 above.

19 HALES, see Note 1 above.

20 HALES, see Note 1 above.

21 BOYATZIS R. *The Competent Manager*. New York, Wiley, 1982.

2 The conduct of managerial work

Managerial work as described in the last chapter is indeed fragmented, but the effective management of diverse activities still requires managers to exercise a number of skills in order to achieve their goals. In fact, these skills become even more important as a means of maintaining some order in what could otherwise be chaos.

On completing this chapter, a reader will understand and be able to explain the managerial skills concerned with:

- planning, prioritising and organising work

- carrying out the work – directing (which includes the agreement of objectives), allocating tasks, delegating, co-ordinating and implementing

- controlling work, including monitoring and evaluating.

The other basic skills given detailed consideration in succeeding chapters are: working for other people (Chapter 3), communicating (Chapter 4), working in teams (Chapter 5), and conducting meetings (Chapter 6).

PLANNING

Planning is the process of deciding on a course of action, ensuring that the resources required to implement the action will be available, and scheduling the programme of work required to achieve a defined end-result.

Planning activities

The main activities are:

- *objective-setting* – deciding what needs to be achieved over a certain timescale

- *activity analysis* – deciding what will have to be done in order to achieve the objective

- *forecasting* – assessing how much work will have to be done, how the workload might change, and how likely it is that any specialised or rush jobs that might have to be undertaken might also require a reassessment of the plan

- *scheduling* – determining the sequence and timescales of the operations and events required to produce results within the deadline: this involves deciding on priorities (prioritisation) – a key managerial activity

- *resourcing* – deciding how many and what sort of people will be required, and when; assessing demands for finance, facilities, materials and bought-in parts in terms of amounts, types and when they need to be available

- *procedure planning* – deciding how the work will be carried out

- *setting targets and standards* – for output, sales, times, quality, costs, and for any other aspects of work where performance and progress need to be monitored and controlled

- *setting up monitoring procedures* – deciding on performance measures and instituting methods for monitoring and controlling performance and progress.

Winston Churchill once said that 'It is wise to plan ahead but only as far as you can see.' What are the implications of this statement for managers?

It has been argued that there is nothing special about planning – it is only a matter of thinking systematically and using common sense. What do you think of this statement?

Managers have been known to say 'What's the point of planning? You're always overtaken by events.' What do you think of this comment?

You have been put in charge of a project to commission and build a new warehouse on a 'green-field' site for a publishing company to store about 250,000 books and from which the company will distribute books to wholesalers and retailers on demand. What are the initial steps you would take?

PRIORITISING

The prioritising of work involves deciding on the relative importance of a range of demands or tasks so that the order in which they are then undertaken can be determined. The fragmented nature of managerial work (as described in Chapter 1) and the sudden and often conflicting demands made on managers' time means that managers are constantly faced with decisions on when to do things. They may often find themselves in a situation where they have to cope with conflicting priorities. This can be stressful unless they adopt a systematic approach to prioritisation.

Prioritisation can be carried out in stages.

1 List all the things you have to do. These can be classified in three groups:
  - regular duties, such as submitting a report, calling on customers, carrying out a performance review
  - special requests from managers, colleagues, customers, clients, suppliers etc delivered orally, by telephone, letter, fax or e-mail
  - self-generated work, such as preparing proposals on an innovation.

2 Classify each item on the list according to
  - the significance of the task to be done in terms of its impact on your work (and reputation) and on the results achieved by the organisation, your team or anyone else involved
  - the importance of the person requesting the work or expecting you to deliver something: less significant tasks may well be put higher on the priority list if they are set by the chief executive or a key client
  - the urgency of the tasks – deadlines, what will happen if it is not completed on time
  - any scope there may be for extending deadlines, altering start and finish times and dates
  - how long each task will take to complete, noting any required or imposed starting and completion times that cannot be changed.

3 Assess how much time you have available to complete the tasks, apart from the routine work which you must get done. Also assess what resources, such as your own staff, are available to get the work done.

4 Draw up a provisional list of priorities by reference to the criteria of significance, importance and urgency listed at Stage 2 above.

5 Assess the possibility of fitting this prioritised schedule of work into the time available. If it proves difficult, put self-imposed priorities on a back-burner and concentrate on the significant tasks. Negotiate for completion or delivery times where you believe they are possible, and when successful, move those tasks down the priority list.

6 Finalise the list of priorities and schedule the work you have to do (or you have to get others to do) accordingly.

Set out step-by-step like this, prioritisation looks a formidable task. But experienced managers go through all these stages almost unconsciously, although systematically, whenever they are confronted with a large workload or conflicting priorities. What many of them do is simply write out a 'Things to do' list at the beginning of the week, or quickly run through in their minds all the considerations described in the above six-stage sequence and make notes on a piece of paper.

You are the personnel manager of a manufacturing plant based in the Midlands which is part of an American-owned engineering company. You report directly to the plant manager but you are functionally responsible to the group personnel director. On your return from two weeks holiday on 5 July you find the following e-mail messages:

1 *From the plant manager*
- We're running into services problems getting contract A5612 out on time. There is a serious shortage of skilled assemblers on that project. Contact me as soon as you return. (2 July.)
- The union has put in a pay claim for a 'substantial increase'. They want to hold a preliminary meeting with

us on 9 July. We shall need to discuss our response. (30 June.)

- You didn't let me have your proposals on the new pay structure before you went on holiday, although I understand they are just about complete. We really need to get on with this. Please contact me on your return. (23 June.)

2 *From the group personnel manager*
- The director of Comp and Ben from the States is joining our group personnel conference on 7 July. He would like to hear your ideas about a new pay structure in your plant; so would everyone else. I should like you to make a presentation – 30 minutes or so. (28 June.)

3 *From the production manager*
- I had to suspend John Smith of the Assembly Shop on Wednesday, 30 June for fighting. I didn't want to take immediate action pending an enquiry in which I think you should take part – there are complications. But the shop steward has complained to me that nothing has happened yet. We need to get on with the enquiry as soon as you return. (2 July.)
- I am worried about the shortage of skilled assemblers – it's holding up work. Can we discuss when you return? (1 July.)

4 *From the sales manager*
- Karen Brown, one of my best reps, has just told me that she's been offered a much better job (a 20 per cent increase in salary). I really need to keep her – she looks after one of our key clients. Can we discuss this urgently when you are back? (30 June.)

5 *From Bill Robinson*
- You interviewed me for the position of progress co-ordinator on 18 June but I have heard nothing since then. I should like to know the outcome of the interview. (1 July.)

6 *From your secretary*
- Ruby Sharpe came into my office in tears today saying that she has been harassed by her manager. I think you should see her as soon as possible after your return. (23 June.)
- Group is pestering me for our personnel return which they said should have been with them on 24 June. Can you give it to me to send to them on Monday? (2 July.)

> You have left Monday and Tuesday free before you attend the two-day group personnel conference which is to be held in Central London on Wednesday and Thursday, 7 and 8 July (a three-line whip commands your presence).
>
> What approach will you adopt to sorting out your priorities?

ORGANISING

Organising involves dividing the overall management task into a variety of processes and activities, and then establishing the means of ensuring that they are carried out effectively. As a manager you have to decide who does what in your team. This may not involve a grand re-design very frequently, if at all, but it may be necessary to make frequent adjustments in response to changes in activities, demands and people.

Organising means defining who does what (teams and individuals) and establishing reporting relationships between them. It is also concerned with deciding how activities should be co-ordinated and controlled and the means of communication that will be used.

Your aim will be to clarify roles, accountabilities (responsibilities for results), relationships and expectations so far as this is possible in fluid, even turbulent, conditions. You will also need to ensure that people are given the scope and opportunity to use their skill to good effect and to develop their competencies.

Organisation design is considered more fully in Chapter 9.

DIRECTING

Managers are there to set the direction, to ensure that their function, department or team is moving purposefully towards a defined goal. But this should not be regarded as a process of simply commanding people to do what they are told. Good managers are not in the business of requiring compliance. They should seek willing co-operation rather than grudging submission. They need to involve people in deciding what needs to be done and how it should be done. Managers should see themselves as facilitators rather than commanders.

But it is still necessary to provide a sense of direction, to get people to understand where the organisation and their team are heading, and the part they are expected to play in getting there. Directing is therefore about furthering understanding and agreement on where the team and its members are expected to go. It is a key aspect of leadership. As Kotter[1] wrote:

> The direction-setting aspect of leadership does not produce plans: it creates visions and strategies. These describe a business, technology or corporate culture in terms of what it should become over the long term and articulate a feasible way of achieving the goal.

> Charles Handy[2] has written that 'A leader shapes and shares a vision which gives point to the work of others.' What is the implication of this statement for the 'directing' aspect of a manager's job?

Specifically, a sense of direction can be achieved by agreeing objectives and targets.

Agreeing objectives

An objective is something which is to be accomplished. For individuals or teams, objectives express what they are expected to achieve. A target is a quantified objective. But objectives can also be defined in qualitative terms as standards of performance. These set out the levels of performance required in a statement such as 'Performance in this area will be at the required standard when ... (something specified happens).'

A performance standard could therefore be expressed like this:

• Performance will be up to standard when callers are dealt with courteously at all times, whatever the circumstances.

Objectives should be agreed rather than 'set'. The latter word implies a top-down command: 'This is your objective because I say it is.' Agreement is important because commitment to achieving objectives is much more likely to exist when individuals and teams have taken part in formulating objectives which they believe they can reasonably be expected to achieve. It is, however, a joint process. Managers must have their say. They have to meet the challenge set by the overall corporate objectives. It is up to them to present to their teams the challenge to which they are expected to respond, but also to listen to their views about what realistically can be done.

The agreement of objectives should be a top-down *and* bottom-up process. The top-down aspect is what management wants achieved; the bottom-up part is what individuals and teams believe they can achieve. The top-down views may ultimately prevail in general terms because, for example, management may have no choice but to take steps to increase shareholder value because of pressure from institutional investors who have the power to demand better returns on their investment. But the work objectives of teams and individuals may be modified to take account of their particular circumstances as long as, overall, they will be contributing sufficiently to the achievement of the goals of the business.

The process of agreeing objectives need not be unduly complicated. It should start from an agreed list of key result areas or main activities. It is then simply a matter of jointly examining each area and agreeing targets or standards of performance as appropriate.

Some organisations use the acronym SMART to define a good objective:

S – stretching/specific
M – measurable
A – agreed
R – realistic
T – time-related

The following problems can arise in agreeing objectives:
- It may be difficult to define specific and meaningful targets.
- Where quantified targets cannot be set, it may be difficult to define qualitative standards.
- Individuals may not be prepared to accept the targets or standards their managers think they should be set for their jobs.
- Individuals may agree too readily to targets or objectives without thinking through how they are going to attain them, and as a result may fail.

How would you deal with these problems?

Charles Handy[3] advocates the creation of a 'culture of consent'. What does he mean by this, and how can it be achieved?

Targets

A target is a quantified and time-based objective. It defines measurable outputs and when they have to be achieved. The target may be to attain a specific level of output or to improve performance by a given amount. Targets can be expressed in financial terms, such as profits to be made, income to be generated, costs to be reduced, or budgets to be worked within. Or they may be expressed in numerical terms, as a number of units to be processed, sales to be achieved, responses to be obtained or customers to be contacted over a period of time.

Direction as the processes of allocating work and delegating

Managers have to define their own objectives as well as those of the members of their teams. They have then to manage their own workload. But if, in the familiar phrase, managing is getting things done through people, they must also be concerned with allocating and delegating work to other people in the light of agreed objectives and targets. They would not be managers if they could do it all themselves. They have to get contributions from other people if they are to achieve their overall task.

ALLOCATING WORK

Allocating work means assigning it to a person or a group of people in order to achieve a purpose. Managers are usually responsible for a related group of activities. They cannot do them all on their own. They need to allocate them – dividing the overall task into a number of subsidiary tasks, defining what they are, what has to be achieved, and how it is to be achieved.

The process of allocating work

The process of allocating work is carried out in stages.

1 Define the overall task – what the unit, section or team is there to do.

2 Analyse the activities required to achieve the task.

3 Decide how best to allocate the activities – to individuals or amongst groups of individuals. This is the process of organisation design as described in Chapter 9.

4 Define the tasks which teams or individuals have to carry out. Each task should ideally consist of three elements: planning, executing and controlling. If this can be achieved, the work is likely to be more satisfying and motivating to the team or individuals and you will get better results. You aim should be to empower the individual or the team as far as you can. Empowerment gives people singly and in groups more scope or 'power' to exercise control over and take responsibility for their work. It provides greater space for individuals to use their abilities or teams to deploy their collective skills to take decisions close to the point of impact – for example, handling a customer query or complaint. (Allocating work to teams is discussed in more detail in Chapter 5, and individual job design is covered in Chapter 9.)

5 Define and explain the purpose of the tasks to the people who will carry them out. It is important for them to understand how what they do contributes to

the achievement of the overall purpose of their department or team and to the achievement of the purposes of other related activities. (This is particularly important when horizontal processes are cutting across organisational boundaries.)

6 Define expectations of the standards of performance required and any quantitative targets that must be achieved. As far as possible these expectations should be discussed and agreed with the people or team concerned – it is important that they have a sense of 'ownership': 'This is what we have agreed to; we believe we are capable of doing it; we're going to do it.' Targets and standards should be defined so as to be related to (integrated with) organisational or functional objectives and the organisation's standards and core values.

7 Agree performance measures which indicate how well the individual or team performs in carrying out the task and achieving targets and standards. Performance measures can relate to such criteria as work, quality, output, timelines (delivery or completion on line, speed of reaction or turnaround) and income/costs. The aim should be to place people in a position in which by referring to each of the measures they can use information on performance to control their own work.

8 Agree any procedures to be used for measuring and reporting on progress and performance.

9 Define the skills and competences needed to achieve a satisfactory level of performance, and make arrangements as required for individuals to acquire or develop these skills.

10 Emphasise that people will be encouraged to think out for themselves the best way to carry out the work wherever there is any choice. Indicate also that you will encourage and welcome any suggestions on how work methods could be improved or how the allocation of work could be altered for the better.

> You are a manager in an insurance company where the present arrangement is that the work is divided into four sections: processing initial enquiries about insurance policies, amending existing policies, underwriting new policies, and dealing with bad claims. The company has decided to focus attention more on customer service and has asked you to form teams of people who will deal with all these activities jointly for groups of customers from different regions. How do you set about allocating work to the newly formed teams?

Giving instructions

The process of allocating work is concerned with the permanent or at least longer-term distribution of duties and tasks to people. But on a day-to-day basis you will certainly need to get new or different things done by individual members of your team or by the team as a whole. What you then have to do is to define and agree

- what has to be done

- why it has to be done

- how it has to be done (if it is new or different)

- what resources are available to do it (people, money, materials, time)

- what results are expected

- when it has to be done

- how you and everyone else involved will know that it has been done (performance indicators).

The more you can involve people in reaching agreement with you under each of these headings the better. It is particularly important to get their views about how they will do the work. Every time you give an instruction, a learning opportunity is created. People will learn much better if they are encouraged to think through for themselves the best way to do something. This is called 'self-managed learning' and it is the best form of learning. Of course, you may have to provide some guidance and help, and you may have to arrange for special training.

But if people are encouraged to do their own thing they will learn faster and be more capable of getting on with it themselves. Your aim should be to minimise the amount of close supervision you have to exercise. This frees you for more important planning, development and monitoring activities, and for liaising and networking with your colleagues.

> You have an experienced assistant buyer in your team who is efficient in the basic task of placing and processing orders with suppliers. However, as part of a total quality management programme it has been decided that buyers should be more involved in specifying and monitoring quality standards. How do you approach instructing your assistant buyer in these new duties?

DELEGATING

Delegation is defined by the *Oxford English Dictionary* as 'the commitment of authority or power' to someone. Delegation involves giving people the authority to do something rather than doing it yourself.

You delegate work when you want someone else to do something because you do not have the time to do it yourself, or because you do not want to do it yourself (for good reasons – because you have more important things to do, *not* because you want to get rid of a tedious task!), or because there is someone who can carry out the task better than you can, or because delegation is one of the best ways of developing and motivating people – extending their skills and increasing their sense of responsibility and confidence in themselves.

To summarise, you delegate when

- you have more work than you can effectively carry out yourself

- you cannot allocate yourself sufficient time for your priority tasks

- you believe the task can be done adequately by the individual (or even better if he or she has expertise you do not have)

- you want to develop the skills and competencies of the individual

- you want to empower the individual, giving him or her more scope and authority to do things without reference back to you.

Delegation can be distinguished from work allocation. Delegation involves relinquishing part of your own authority – something that you are accountable for – to someone else. When work is delegated to people, they receive authority to do things which they previously did not have. But you cannot delegate responsibility, for ultimately you are accountable for the actions of the people to whom you have delegated work.

Work allocation is the process of defining what people are expected to do to carry out their role on a continuing basis. From time to time they will be allocated specific tasks – given instructions – but these will not be activities which you would normally be expected to carry out yourself. Yet the distinction between giving instructions and delegating is a fine one.

The process of delegation

When you delegate you have to decide:

- *what to delegate* – You delegate tasks that you do not need to do yourself or tasks which will develop the skills of people or enhance their sense of responsibility for what they are doing. You may also delegate work to those with particular expertise. You will generally know what needs to be done and how it should be done, but others may have in-depth knowledge which you cannot be expected to possess. The ability to make the best use of specialists through delegation is one of the hallmarks of an effective manager.

- *who does the work* – Ideally, the person you select should have the knowledge, skills, motivation, confidence and time to get the work done to your complete satisfaction. But you may have to choose someone who does not meet the ideal specification. In which case, identify someone with the basic attributes and the willingness to learn to do the work with your help and guidance. This is how people develop, and the development of people should be your conscious aim whenever you delegate. You will also be looking for people you can trust to get on with it – you do not want to be constantly breathing down their necks. You can find out who can be trusted by progressively trying people out, first on relatively small and unimportant tasks and then by giving them increasingly more scope. With inexperienced or untested people, start by relinquishing relatively little of your authority and limiting their freedom to act independently. Progressively thereafter, give them more scope until finally they have almost complete freedom to do the work.

- *how to give out the work* – Basically, your approach to delegating work should follow the pattern of giving instructions described earlier in this chapter. A distinction can be made between 'hard' and 'soft' delegation. Hard delegation takes place when you tell someone what to do, how to do it, and when you want the results. Soft delegation takes place when you agree generally what has to be achieved and leave the individual to get on with it. You still need to agree limits of authority, define any decisions which should be referred to you, and indicate when and how you will review progress. Whether a soft or a hard approach is adopted, you should always delegate by the results you expect.

- *how you can guide and develop* – Delegation not only helps you to get your own work done, it also helps to develop skills and confidence and increase the degree to which you can trust people to take on additional tasks with more freedom to act. Guidance, helping people to learn, and coaching are all parts of the process of delegating.

You may also have to provide specific guidance to relatively inexperienced people at the start of a task. And, without interfering unduly, you should be prepared to provide guidance as necessary. Your role is not to let your people sink or swim. You have to keep them afloat. Remember, however, that there is a delicate balance to be maintained between undue interference and helpful guidance. This distinction may be difficult. But delegation, although important, is never an easy option – you have to work at it.

• *how to monitor performance* – At first you may have to monitor performance fairly carefully if someone is new to the task. But the sooner you can relax and watch progress informally, the better. You have to try to restrain yourself from undue interference in the way the work is being done. You do not want people to make mistakes, but you can help them to learn from them if they do occur. And you have to accept that some mistakes are likely – this is where trust is important. There should be an understanding that people should come to you in good time before things get out of hand. There should be no recriminations – rather congratulations that you have been informed. A joint problem-solving approach can then be adopted in which agreement is reached on the cause of the problem, what can be done about it now, and what can be done to prevent its recurrence in the future. That is what is meant by allowing people to learn from their mistakes.

The capacity to trust someone to do something well is an important requirement for effective delegation. How do you build up your trust in other people? How can you ensure that people learn to trust you?

The phrase 'delegate by the results you expect' was used earlier: how can you do this in practice?

The phenomenon of 'river-banking' has been described as what happens when a boss delegates something that is very difficult to do without proper guidance or help. As the individual is going down in the river for the third time, the boss is observed in a remote and safe position on the river bank saying 'It's easy, really. All you need to do is to try a bit harder.' What should you do to avoid river-banking?

CO-ORDINATING

Co-ordination is the process of ensuring that the tasks carried out by people are integrated so that they mesh together to achieve a common purpose through unified effort. Activities cannot be carried out in isolation. They have to be linked together so that they are conducted in the required sequence or in conjunction with one another. Organisations have to distinguish, or differentiate, the various activities required to achieve their purpose, but they also have to integrate these activities so that the required flow of work is maintained between different areas of operation. It may be furthered by a business process re-engineering exercise which, obviously, is concerned with business processes – the combination or sequence of activities that takes one or more kinds of input and creates an output that is of value to the customer. In this way order fulfilment may be seen as a process which starts with one order as the input and results in the delivery of the ordered goods. The various activities at each stage in this process need to be sequenced and co-ordinated to ensure that all happens according to plan.

Why co-ordinate?

Co-ordination is required because individual actions may need to be synchronised. Activities must follow each other in sequence. Others must be carried out simultaneously in order that all elements of the enterprise finish together. People may want to do their own thing. Initiative and a spirit of independence are desirable qualities – yet if people who display them do not contribute alongside the efforts of others to achieve the goal, they may or may not be wasting their own time but they definitely will be hindering the achievement of the required end-result.

What co-ordination involves

Co-ordination involves getting people to work together. In general it means integrating activities, exercising leadership, and team-building (see Chapter 5). It also means carrying out specific activities:

- *planning* – Co-ordination should take place before the event. This means deciding what needs to be done, and when. It also means sequencing activities through processes such as networks and deciding when they have to be carried out jointly and how the mutual support required is to be provided.

- *organising* – When dividing work between teams and people, avoid breaking apart those tasks which are linked together and which you cannot separate clearly from one another. You have to identify potential barriers between related activities and get rid of them by emphasising that the sequence of work is a continuous process and that all concerned have a responsibility not only for carrying out the work in their own area but also for ensuring that it flows smoothly into the next area. People must be encouraged to appreciate that they must link up with other people – co-ordinated teamwork should be emphasised as a core value, and the ability to work well in a team should be an important factor in assessing performance.

- *communicating* – You should not only communicate what you expect people to do but also convey the importance you attach to your staff's communicating with each other. They key to effective co-ordination is good communication.

- *monitoring* – The steps listed above should help to enhance co-ordination but they cannot guarantee that it will happen. Managers need to monitor what is going on and take swift action if there is evidence of poor co-ordination.

> What do you think are likely to be the main barriers to achieving good co-ordination? How would you overcome them?

IMPLEMENTING

Implementing is about making things happen – achieving the expected results. Effective achievers – implementers – have specific characteristics:

- They define to themselves precisely what they want to do.

- They set themselves realistic but reachable goals that may nonetheless extend them somewhat.

- They set demanding but not unattainable timescales in which to do it.

- They convey clearly what they expect.

- They carry their teams with them by the quality of their leadership.

- They are prepared to discuss how things should be done and will listen to, and take, advice. But once a course of action has been agreed, they stick to it unless external events or pressures dictate a change of direction.

- They are single-minded about getting where they want to go, sharing perseverance and determination in the face of adversity.

- They demand high performance from themselves as well as from everyone else.

- They work hard and well under pressure – in fact, it brings out the best in them.

- They tend to be dissatisfied with the *status quo*.

- They are never completely satisfied with their own performance and continually question themselves.

- They take calculated risks.

- They snap out of setbacks without being personally shattered, and quickly regroup their forces and their ideas.

- They are enthusiastic about what they do and convey their enthusiasm to others.

- They are decisive – they are able quickly to sum up situations, define and agree alternative courses of action, determine the preferred course.

CONTROLLING

Controlling is about monitoring and measuring performance, comparing results with plans, and taking corrective action when required. But control is not simply a matter of putting things right. Control is relative. It is concerned with comparing the difference between planned and actual performance. It also has a positive side – getting more or better things done on the basis of information received. Good control is dependent on monitoring and evaluation processes (as discussed later in this section).

Exercising control

To exercise good control you need to

- *plan* what you aim to achieve

- *measure* regularly what has been achieved

- *compare* actual achievements with the plan

- *take action* to correct deviations from the plan or to develop opportunities revealed by the information.

Control need not be oppressive. You should not make people feel that you are watching them all the time, waiting for them to make a mistake. In fact, you should do everything possible to get them to control themselves – to monitor their own performances and take action as required. Self-control is far better than top-down command and control.

Setting up a control system

In accordance with the points above, it is preferable to involve people in setting up their own control system.

This is one of the ways in which empowerment can be achieved. Your main task will then be to guide them on two essential requirements:

- how to set appropriate and fair targets, standards and budgets

- how to decide what information is required for control purposes and ensure that it is made available in a readily assimilated form, in good time, and to the right people (ie those carrying out the work) so that they can take action – control information should be the property of the team, not just the team leader.

What problems is a manager likely to meet when setting up a control system? How might they be overcome?
How can a manager encourage people to carry out their own procedures?
How can a manager retain overall control while simultaneously delegating authority to people to carry out and monitor their own performance?

Monitoring

To exercise control, managers have to be continuously aware of what is going on in their departments or teams. They must know how well their unit is performing against its objectives and how well individual team members are performing. Monitoring is the process of measuring and observing what is happening as it happens so that action can be taken as required – swiftly if need be. Managers should also monitor their own performance against plans, budgets, objectives and standards.

Effective monitoring requires managers initially to define or establish clearly the plan or programme they have to implement, the targets and standards of performance they have to achieve, and the budgets within which they have to operate. They should then identify the performance measures they can use for monitoring purposes. These can be classified under several headings:

- *Finance* – income, shareholder value, added value, rates of return, costs

- *Output* – units produced or processed, throughput, new accounts

- *Impact* – attainment of a standard (quality, level of service, etc), changes in behaviour (internal and external customers), completion of work/project, level of take-up of a service, innovation

- *Reaction* – judgement by others, colleagues, internal and external customers

- *Time* – speed of response or turnaround, achievements compared with timetables, amount of backlog, time to market, delivery times.

The next step is to identify the feedback information that will be available to measure performance. This may be control data generated by the process itself, management reports based on data collection, direct feedback of results from returns or observations, or personal feedback from individuals in the form of progress or activity reports.

Finally, monitoring means comparing feedback information with plans, targets or budgets, and evaluating results as a basis for action (as described below).

Evaluating

Evaluating follows monitoring. It involves analysing, gauging and appraising outcomes. A diagnosis is made of the causes of any problems and of the issues that need to be addressed. The analysis and diagnosis provide the basis for planning – to make the best use of opportunities or to deal with weaknesses or threats. Evaluation may require an assessment of the pros and cons of alternative courses of action in order to come to a balanced decision on what needs to be done and the priorities that should be attached to the various tasks involved.

SUMMARY

Planning

- Planning involves deciding what to do, getting the resources required, and scheduling work.

- The main planning activities are: objective-setting, activity analysis, forecasting, scheduling, resourcing, procedure-planning, setting targets and standards, and deciding on monitoring procedures.

Prioritising

- Prioritisation means deciding on the relative importance of tasks so that the order in which they should be done can be determined.

- Prioritisation can be carried out by listing things to do, classifying them in terms of their significance, importance and urgency, assessing how much time is available, and fitting the scheduled tasks into this timescale.

Organising

- Organising means analysing what has to be done and then deciding who does what, setting up the reporting relationships between people, and establishing methods of communication, co-ordination and control.

Directing

- Direction is concerned with getting understanding and agreement on where the team and its members are expected to go – ie their objectives and targets.

- Direction means agreeing objectives and targets, and allocating and delegating work.

Delegating

- Delegation involves giving people the authority to do something rather than doing it yourself.

- Managers delegate when they do not have the time to do everything themselves.

- Delegation means that individuals can develop their skills and competencies.

- Delegation involves empowerment – giving people more scope and authority.

- When delegating, you must decide what to delegate and to whom. You have to select people who are capable of doing work immediately or with a reasonable amount of guidance.

- A distinction can be made between 'hard' delegation – giving people full instructions on what to do – and 'soft' delegation – indicating what people have to do and letting them get on with it.

- You should always delegate by the results you expect, and set up arrangements for monitoring and reporting on performance.

Co-ordinating

- Co-ordination involves the achievement of unity of effort so that individual actions are synchronised and sequenced properly.

- Co-ordinating requires planning and scheduling activities, organising work so that it can be co-ordinated, communicating and monitoring.

Implementing

- Implementing is about making things happen.

- Effective implementers know what they want done and provide the guidance and leadership necessary to ensure that it does get done.

Controlling

- Controlling is concerned with monitoring and measuring performance, comparing results with plans, and taking corrective action if and when required.

- To exercise good control it is necessary to plan, monitor, measure, evaluate, compare, and take action.

REFERENCES

1 KOTTER J. 'Power, dependence and effective management', *Harvard Business Review*, July–August 1971.
2 HANDY C. *Understanding Organisations*, Harmondsworth, Penguin Books, 1985.
3 HANDY, see Note 2 above.

3 Working for other people

Working for other people means responding to objectives, meeting deadlines, delivering completed and acceptable work, and dealing with your boss.

At the end of this chapter, a reader will understand:

- how to respond to the expectations and requirements of your boss (agreeing and achieving objectives)

- how to deliver completed and acceptable work

- how to meet deadlines

- how to deal with difficult bosses

- how to manage your boss.

The next chapter deals with further aspects of working for others in terms of communications, influencing techniques, report-writing and making presentations.

RESPONDING TO EXPECTATIONS

The contemporary concept of 'the psychological contract' tends to arouse expectations in bosses about how their staff should behave and perform, and expectations in staff about how their bosses should treat them. But these mutual expectations may not only be unwritten, they may be no more than assumptions. On the other hand, where there is a more formal approach to performance management, objectives and standards of performance will have been agreed. This section of the chapter considers responses to the unwritten (psychological) contract. The next section covers managing the agreement of expectations – setting and agreeing objectives.

The psychological contract
From the point of view of most managers, the psychological

contract between them and their staff implies that the latter should display specific behaviours and characteristics:

- competence

- effort

- commitment

- willingness

- compliance

- loyalty.

Expectations of competence, effort and commitment are not unreasonable. You should receive guidance, support and coaching from your manager, but in the last analysis it is up to you to develop your competencies or capabilities and deliver results accordingly. This is the principle of self-directed learning. People learn most effectively if they take responsibility for identifying and meeting their own learning needs. You can ask for guidance and help, and your organisation may have a personal development planning process which structures your learning endeavours and programmes. What you have to do for yourself, however, is to review how well you are doing your work, to identify what you need to learn in order to do your work better, and to take steps to acquire the knowledge and skills you need with whatever help you can get from your boss, your colleagues and the organisation.

It is equally reasonable for your boss to expect you to direct the required amount of effort to getting the work done. People may be criticised for being incompetent but they will be damned once it is believed that they are lazy.

Commitment is also a reasonable expectation. Commitment requires that you demonstrate your identification with the goals of the organisation and of your area of operation, that you actively support the values of the organisation, that you show a desire to remain part of the organisation (you are not constantly and obviously looking for another job), and that you demonstrate by your actions and behaviour that you are prepared to put yourself out on behalf of the organisation, your boss and the colleagues in your team. If someone says of you that you are fully committed, then that is praise indeed.

Willingness could be regarded as evidence of commitment but is rather more problematic. It is not reasonable for your boss to expect blind obedience, but it makes bosses happy if, when they ask someone to do something extra or special, the response is 'Yes, I'll do my best' (unless the task is clearly impossible). What bosses do not want to hear is endless grumbles following quite proper and reasonable requests to do something. A sullen and grudging acquiescence is almost as bad.

Where the expectations are of compliance or blind loyalty they become even more problematic. To demand compliance is in effect to say 'You will do what I tell you to do – or else.' It is a process of bending someone else's will: 'But me no buts.' There will, of course, be occasions when bosses can reasonably say 'Look, this is important. I'd like you to drop everything and get on with this.' They may be under equally strong or even greater pressure from above. But these should be *rare occasions* not a habitual approach which requires instant obedience. Martinet bosses like this still exist, even in these more easy-going and democratic days.

Finally, there is loyalty. It is reasonable to expect people to be loyal to their bosses, in the sense of providing support and not indulging in snide criticisms or comments to other people. But blind and unswerving loyalty upwards cannot be demanded. It should never be the case that 'I shall be loyal to my boss through thick and thin, right or wrong.' Bosses who behave impossibly and make impossible demands, bosses who refuse to recognise good work, do not deserve loyalty. And loyalty is a two-way process. If bosses are not loyal to their staff (supporting and developing them, trying to provide security), why should their staff be loyal to them?

This issue extends to organisations as well as bosses. Organisations expect commitment and loyalty from their staff – but do they display any commitment and loyalty in return? Some do; others don't. To make people redundant at the first sign of a business problem, to downsize or (an even worse euphemism) to 'rightsize', is hardly displaying the characteristics of commitment and loyalty they demand from their employees.

> What do *you* think bosses can reasonably expect from their staff?

RESPONDING TO OBJECTIVES

Bosses are in the business of managing for performance. They will have to respond to the targets and objectives set at the top of the organisation, which management will want to 'cascade' down to ensure that at every level the contribution expected of people towards the achievement of the overall purpose of the business is understood and agreed. This is the process of integrating objectives, and each boss will want to ensure that this happens within his or her own area.

Cascading objectives is a top-down process, but there should be a bottom-up element which provides for people to make proposals on what they believe they can achieve and to comment on what their bosses say they are expected to achieve. Clearly, there is room for disagreement here, but it is one of the key skills of a manager to achieve consensus on what he or she believes or is told is necessary and what the staff believe they can deliver. Bosses will want to get people to accept objectives that extend them because of the thrust for continuous performance improvement. Some people will resist unreasonably; others may have valid points to make about what it is possible for them to achieve. When they are indeed valid, it is up to the boss to agree to modifications, subject to the agreement of higher authority. If the latter is not forthcoming, the boss may have to say in effect: 'That's the way it is. I would like you to do your best.'

To work well with your boss you may have to accept that this kind of thing will happen from time to time. What you should not do is to raise unreasonable or frivolous objections. Your boss may be equipped with benchmark information which shows that the expected targets or standards are being achieved by people within the business or in other organisations. You would have to make out a good case to confront this sort of data.

If there is a formal process for agreeing objectives and standards – as there should be – then your part in it should have been defined by those setting up the process. Where it has not been defined you can always ask politely if it can be done.

Typically, before a meeting to agree objectives you will be asked if you would come to a conclusion about what your key result areas are. (These should have been formally defined in a job description. If they are not in your job description, make sure that they become part of it forthwith.) Having listed these areas, the next thing to consider is what targets (output, service delivery, response time, etc) can be set in quantified terms, and what standards of performance you should be expected to achieve in any area in which quantified targets cannot be set. A standard of performance is a statement of the expected behaviour and the conditions that will exist when a task has been well done. If you have carried out this exercise before, you can look at the targets and standards agreed last year and assess how you have got on with them. This will give you a lead towards what new targets or standards may be set. In some cases no changes need be made. This process of self-assessment is used as the basis for performance review in some company schemes.

As well as setting new or revised targets, this pre-meeting analysis on your part can include some thought on how you are going to achieve the targets and what help you will need from your manager – guidance, support, coaching, or the provision of extra resources. This gives you an opportunity to express your expectations of what you want your boss to do for you.

Performance reviews should be a two-way process which provide for the definition and agreement of mutual expectations. In many organisations there is no such provision for this exchange of views although it is a potentially productive process. Good bosses will recognise that they can learn from their staff just as their staff can learn from them. In one sense managers' teams are composed of their internal customers who have the right to expect proper leadership, guidance and support.

> 'Bosses are there to give orders; subordinates are there to obey instructions.' What is your reaction to this statement?

RESPONDING TO OBJECTIVES

Managers take part in agreeing objectives with their own bosses as well as with the people who report to them. In objective-agreement sessions they have to find answers to such questions as:

- What are the key result areas of my job? (A key result area is a critical part of the job which strongly influences the achievement of its overall purpose.)

- What objectives can I set for each of these key result areas? Each objective will define what I have to achieve in terms of targets or standards of performance.

- Are these objectives SMART? That is, are they *s*tretching/*s*pecific, *m*easurable, likely to be *a*greed, *r*ealistic and *t*ime-related?

- How do these objectives support the achievement of the objectives of the organisation? The aim should be to align individual and organisational objectives.

- What are the critical success factors that will affect the achievement of the objectives? Critical success factors are the parts of a job which make a particularly significant contribution to the achievement of its overall purpose and for which objectives can be set. Defining them indicates the areas to which most attention needs to be given and what elements of work need to be measured, monitored and evaluated.

- What resources do I need? Resources might include people, money, equipment, materials, time, and support from your manager.

- What are the budgets and timescales I have to work to? This information indicates what controls have to be maintained over expenditure, and provides the basis for planning and project management.

- How will I and my boss know how well I have done? This requires identifying performance measures.

- How am I going to monitor my work against targets and standards by reference to the performance measures?

- On what basis will I and my manager evaluate my performance?

> Consider your own job or another one with which you are familiar and use the above checklist as a guide to defining objectives.

DELIVERING COMPLETED AND ACCEPTABLE WORK

If you are asked to do something, you should come up with solutions, not problems. You should present a completed proposal with whatever supporting arguments or evidence you need. Bosses want answers, not questions. They want a well-argued proposal based on a thorough analysis of the problem, a diagnosis of the issues to be addressed, recommendations which logically flow from the diagnosis and demonstrably deal with the problem, and a conclusion which sets out the actions required to implement the proposal (an action plan) together with an estimate of the costs involved and the benefits that will accrue to the organisation.

When you have finished your report and studied your recommendations and conclusions, ask yourself the question 'If I were my boss, would I stake my reputation on this piece of work and put my name to it?' If the answer is 'No', tear up your report and do it again. It's incomplete.

MEETING DEADLINES

The ability to meet deadlines is one of the most important qualities managers need to possess when they have to take on a project or carry out a special task. If they are responsible for a project, they are most likely to complete work on time if they

- prepare a project plan and programme that is based on an analysis of the work to be carried out in such a way that it can be sequenced and divided into its constituent elements or tasks

- estimate the time to complete each element or task

- add up the element times to produce a total time (on a complex project network-planning techniques can be used)

- prioritise the tasks

- allocate responsibilities for carrying out each segment of work according to the priorities

- define the deadlines everyone involved has to meet for each part of the project for which they are responsible

- set up information systems which monitor work-in-progress against the programme and the deadlines

- call for regular progress reports

- conduct 'milestone' meetings at critical stages through

the project to assess progress and, if necessary, re-schedule the work

• throughout the project exert all their powers of leadership to motivate their team and maintain their commitment

• keep their boss informed of progress and, realistically, their ability to meet the deadline

• are prepared to apply extra resources (including their own time) if there is slippage in the programme

If in this situation things go horribly wrong and managers come to believe that, whatever they do, the deadline will not be met, they should inform their bosses – it is better to warn them of the problem so that corrective action can be initiated at that level in good time rather than to attempt to hide the unpalatable truth.

When aiming to meet deadlines for yourself, the same principles apply. You have to work out priorities, estimate the time for each task, programme your work, mobilise the resources you require, ensure that you assess progress regularly, initiate swift corrective action as required, and keep your boss informed of how things are going and of any serious problems you are facing.

> What do you think are the most likely problems people face when they have to meet deadlines? How would you overcome them?

HOW TO DEAL WITH DIFFICULT BOSSES

Bosses can make entirely unreasonable demands; they can refuse to give any feedback – positive or otherwise; they can ignore your requests; and they can act as bullies. There are no easy answers to these problems. Managers who behave in any of these ways do not deserve to be managers. It is to be hoped that they will be found out, but in the real world this sort of behaviour can still be accompanied by good results, and this may be all that higher management is looking for.

One thing is certain. No one should have to take bullying or harassment. If this is happening to you, a complaint must be made to the personnel department or to higher management. You can ask for a transfer – but that, of course, does not solve the real problem. The prevalence of bullying in organisations has at last been recognised in recent years, and personnel specialists and their managers are much more likely nowadays to take action, at least to investigate the complaint. This itself may have unpleasant consequences for you – it is the nature of bullies to take it out on people who are not in a position to fight back – but it is better to face these consequences than to put up with the bullying.

The other ways in which bosses behave badly may not be quite as stressful. And the dividing line between a reasonable and an unreasonable demand is not always precise. But you have every right to question an entirely improper demand – although you will have to be certain that you can provide supporting evidence for your belief that it is unreasonable. Again, bosses who persist in making such demands are ineffective managers. If they are not spotted from above, you have the right to make it known that a problem exists, if only by giving it as a reason for a transfer request. (If other people feel the same and can join in your protest, so much the better.)

> Your boss doesn't bully you because he knows you will fight back. But you observe him bullying other people who are not as well placed as you are. What do you do about it?
>
> Your boss keeps on demanding the impossible. You know that he is being unreasonable because no one else in similar positions is expected to do what he expects. What do you do about it?

MANAGING YOUR BOSS

Bosses need managing as much as anyone else. Managers exist to get results. They are not there simply to please their own managers. But they are more likely to get things done and progress in the organisation if they can:

- get agreement from their managers on what they are expected to do

- deal with their managers effectively when problems arise

- impress their managers generally with their efficiency, effectiveness and willingness to put themselves out to get a result.

Getting agreement

Getting agreement from managers involves:

- finding out what they expect – their likes and dislikes, their quirks and prejudices, how they like things presented to them, how they like things to be done

- establishing the best ways, times and places to tackle them with a proposal, request or problem

- avoiding open confrontation. If you can't get your own way at first, return later at a more propitious moment. If you get into an argument, leave an escape route – a way open for them to consent to without having to climb down.

- not trying to achieve too much at once. It is often better to tackle one or two things at a time. Bosses have many other preoccupations and their boredom thresholds are often low. Avoid overwhelming them with detail. They will always prefer a clear-cut proposition supported by arguments which are compelling but limited in number and complexity.

Dealing with problems

If things are going wrong, managers should adopt the following approach with their superiors:

- Keep them informed. Never let them be taken by surprise. Prepare them in advance for any bad news.

- Explain what has happened and why (no excuses), and what you propose to do about it.

- Emphasise that you would like their views on what you propose, as well as their agreement – everyone likes to be consulted.

Impressing your boss

Your boss needs to trust you, to rely upon you, and to believe in your capacity to come up with good ideas and to make things happen. He or she doesn't want to wet-nurse you or to spend time correcting your mistakes or covering up for them.

To succeed in impressing your boss without really trying (it is fatal to push too much), you should

- Always be frank and open. Admit mistakes. Never lie or even be economical with the truth. If there is the faintest suspicion that you are not perfectly straightforward, your boss will never trust you again.

- Aim to help your boss to be right. This does not mean being subservient or time-serving. Recognise, however, that you exist to give support – in the right direction.

- Respond fast to requests on a can-do/will-do basis.

- Not trouble him or her unnecessarily with your problems.

- Provide protection where required. Loyalty is an old-fashioned virtue, but you owe it to your boss. If you cannot be loyal, you should get out from under as quickly as you can.

> Why should you have to manage your boss?
> Is managing bosses just about pleasing them, or is there more to it than that? If so, what is it?

SUMMARY

- It is necessary to clarify mutual expectations – what managers expect from their staff; what staff expect from their managers. It is reasonable for managers to expect competence, effort and commitment. It is unreasonable for them to expect compliance or loyalty unless the latter is two-way.

- Expectations in the form of targets and standards should be agreed by the boss and the individual. The latter should be encouraged to think through what can be achieved and the manager should listen to these suggestions and take account of them, although ultimately it may be necessary to accept that overriding corporate objectives will have to prevail.

- Managers have the right to expect finished work from their staff.

- Managers can be unreasonable, even bullies. The latter behaviour should never be tolerated, and a reasoned response to an unreasonable demand should be made.

- It is necessary for staff to give consideration to how they can best manage their bosses by being aware of expectations and making every effort to meet them.

4 Communicating with other people

A great deal of the fragmented time of managers is spent in communicating with other people. They exert influence, write reports and make presentations. On completing this chapter, a reader will understand and be able to explain how these methods of communication – influencing and persuading, report-writing and making presentations – can be used.

INFLUENCING TECHNIQUES

Managers exert influence – on their bosses, on their colleagues and on their teams. They have to persuade people to do things, possibly against their will. It can be said that the manager's job is 60 per cent getting it right and 40 per cent putting it across.

How are people influenced?

People are influenced by arguments or proposals which are logical and practical, which help them to get their work done better or improve results, and which provide them with a new perspective. They are more likely to be swayed by an argument if they see that the proposal benefits them, and are even more likely to agree if the suggestion accords with their own views or feelings.

How should people be influenced?

It follows that if you want to influence others, possibly against their will, you must not only present powerful, well-balanced and fully-backed-up arguments. You must also take pains to understand each other person's point of view (or the collective view of a group of people) and take account of it in presenting your proposal or idea.

There are four basic influencing skills:

1 *asserting* – This means making your views clear, expressing your views in direct ways. Assertive statements
  – are brief and to the point
  – indicate that you are not hiding behind someone, are speaking for yourself by using such clauses as 'I think that ...', 'I believe that ...', 'I feel that ...' – your beliefs and views are important
  – are not over-weighted with advice
  – use questions to find out the views of others and test reactions to your views
  – distinguish between fact and opinion
  – are expressed positively but not dogmatically
  – indicate that you are aware that other people may have different points of view.

2 *bridging* – Draw out other people's points of view; indicate that you understand what they are getting at; give credit to their good ideas and suggestions; join your views with theirs: 'Well, we both seem to be saying the same things, so let's agree to proceed.'

3 *attracting* – Convey your enthusiasm for your ideas; get people to feel that they are taking part in an exciting project.

4 *observing and listening* – Observe people's reactions and listen to what they say. You need to be able to spot the glassy look in someone's eyes when he or she is bored by what you are saying. You need to detect any feelings of hostility so that you can counter them. It is sometimes a good idea to come out into the open and say 'I don't seem to be getting my case across – what's the problem?'

> Think about a proposal that you want to make to someone who may resist it. How would you set about influencing that person?

PERSUADING SKILLS

The key influencing skill is persuasion – using facts, logic and reason to present your own case, emphasising its strong points, anticipating objections to any apparent weaknesses, and appealing to reason.

The ten rules for persuading others are:

1 *Define your objective.*

2 *Get the facts* – Assemble as much data as possible. Even if you do not use it all it may come in useful later as supporting material.

3 *Marshal your argument* – Your aim should be to ensure that you devise a powerful argument which clearly addresses the problem and which is developed logically and inexorably from the facts. You should assemble the supporting data in a way which substantially supports your conclusion.

4 *Anticipate objections* – When marshalling your arguments and developing your proposition, anticipate any objections that may be raised. You can then either deal with them in your proposition – putting them up so as then to knock them down – or you can prepare yourself for dealing with them if they crop up in discussion. It is often useful to suggest different patterns of action, list the pros and cons for each, and come down firmly in favour of one. There is no harm in admitting that you have made this judgement 'on balance'. You accept that points can be made against your proposal, 'but the points for significantly outweigh those against – for the following reasons ...'.

Remember that there are at least twelve ways of saying No, so prepare to deal with them:
- It won't work.
- It's good in theory but not in practice.
- It will cost too much.
- We've tried it before and it didn't work.
- This is not addressing the real problem.
- The benefits won't be realised until it is too late.

  – This is not the right time.
  – It will set a dangerous precedent.
  – We haven't got the resources to implement it.
  – Our shareholders, managing director, sponsors, trustees, shop stewards, workers, customers, clients, suppliers, sales outlets, sales representatives, agents (etc) won't like it.
  – We need to consult with … (etc) before we go any further.
  – We must spend more time considering the implications of this proposal.

5 *Find out what the other person or people want* – Never underestimate a person's natural resistance to change. But bear in mind that such resistance is proportional not to the total extent of the change but to the extent to which it affects that person. When asked to accept a proposition, the first questions people ask themselves are: 'How does this affect me?' 'What do I stand to lose?' and 'What do I stand to gain?' These questions must be answered before persuasion can start. The key to all persuasion is empathy – seeing your proposition from every other person's point of view. If you can really put yourself into their shoes, you will be able to foresee objections and present your ideas in the way most attractive to them. You must find out how they look at things and what they want. Listen to what they have to say. Don't talk too much. Ask questions. If they ask you a question, reply with another question. Find out what they are after, then present your case in a way that highlights its benefits to them, or at least reduces their objections or fears.

6 *Look for the 'hidden agenda'* – A meeting may be called for a particular purpose, but behind this there may be different and more significant things people want to achieve. Some people, for example, may be more interested in improving their status or extending their authority than in achieving something which benefits the organisation.

7 *Prepare a simple and attractive presentation* – Your

presentation should be as simple and straightforward as possible to emphasise the benefits. Don't bury the selling-points. Lead them in gently so there are no surprises. Anticipate objections.

8 *Make your audience, and especially potential doubters, party to your idea* – Get them to contribute, if at all possible. Find some common ground in order to start off with agreement. Don't antagonise them. Avoid defeating them in arguments. Help to preserve self-esteem. Always leave a way out for them.

9 *Sell the benefits positively* – Show conviction. You are not going to influence anyone if you don't believe in what you are proposing and communicate that belief. To persuade effectively you must spell out the benefits of what you are proposing. What you are proposing may be of less interest to the individuals concerned than the effects of that proposal on them.

10 *Clinch things and take immediate action* – Choose the right moment to clinch the proposal. Make sure that you are not pushing too hard – but when you reach your objective, don't stay and risk losing it. Take prompt follow-up action. There is no point in going to all the trouble of getting agreement if you let things slide afterwards.

REPORT-WRITING

Criteria
A good report has specific characteristics:

• a logical structure

• the use of plain words to convey meaning

• messages presented lucidly, persuasively and, above all, succinctly.

Structure
A report should be structured in a way which ensures that the reader is taken through a sequence of sections which are clearly linked to one another and which proceed

logically from the introduction to the conclusions and recommendations. A typical structure might incorporate the following sections:

The introduction

This explains what the report is about, why the report has been written, its aims, its terms of reference, and why it should be read. If the report is divided into sections, readers should be given an indication of the logic of the structure as a signpost to direct them through the report.

The analysis

This is a factual review of the situation or problem. It could describe the present arrangements, breaking them down into their elements – the main areas for attention. It could refer to data collected as part of the study – the key facts that have been assembled – although too much detail should not be included (such detail might perhaps be attached in an appendix). The analysis would identify the symptoms of any problems and should lead directly to the diagnosis.

The diagnosis

This is prepared by reference to the factual analysis. It sets out the issues to be addressed and establishes the causes of any problems. The diagnosis provides the basis for any recommendations.

Recommendations

The recommendations specify the proposed action(s). They should flow logically and clearly from the analysis and diagnosis. Where there is no obvious solution, alternatives may be presented and evaluated, but a clear recommendation should emerge from this evaluation. An indication should be given of what the recommendation involves, and why and how it addresses the issue(s).

Action plan

The action plan sets out what needs to be done to implement the recommendations. It should identify:

- what precisely will have to be done

- who will be responsible

- the resources required (internal staff, external advice, materials and equipment)

- the estimated costs

- the timescale for implementation

- the programme of work.

Conclusions

The conclusions summarise the main findings (the analysis and diagnosis) and recommendations. An indication of the benefits arising from the proposals should be made (such benefits could be linked to costs in the form of a cost/benefit analysis).

Executive summary

An 'executive summary' of the findings, recommendations and conclusions is helpful if the report is long and/or complex. It concentrates a reader's mind and can serve as an agenda for discussion. The summary should be brief – no more than one side of a sheet of paper – and it should be set out in bullet points.

Plain words

To convey meaning without ambiguity and avoid giving the reader unnecessary trouble, it is advisable, as suggested by Gower[1], to:

- Use no more words than are required to express the meaning: if too many are used, the meaning may be obscured and the reader will become tired. Do not use superfluous adjectives and adverbs, and do not use roundabout phrases where single words would serve.

- Use familiar words rather than academic ones if they express the meaning equally well, for the familiar are more likely to be understood.

- Use short words with a precise meaning rather than those

that are vague, for they obviously serve better to make the meaning clear. In particular, choose concrete words over abstract ones, for they are more likely to have a precise meaning. Too many long words may be off-putting.

• Avoid jargon. If its use is essential, explain what it means in plain language.

Presentation

The way in which the report is presented and written affects its impact and value. The reader should be able to follow the argument easily and not get bogged down in too much detail.

Paragraphs should be short, and each one should be restricted to a single topic. It is helpful to use bullet points in order to list and highlight a series of observations or comments.

In long reports it may be a good idea to number paragraphs for ease of reference. Some people prefer the system which numbers main sections 1, 2, etc, subsections 1.1, 1.2, etc, and sub-subsections 1.1.1, 1.1.2, etc. However, this can be clumsy and distracting. A simpler system, which simplifies cross-referencing, is to number each paragraph – not the headings – 1, 2, 3, etc; sub-paragraphs or tabulations can be indicated as bullet points.

Use headings to guide people on what they are about to read and to help them find their way about the report. Adopt a visibly distinctive hierarchy to separate main headings from lesser headings. Main headings might for example be in bold capitals or bold upper and lower case, and subheadings might be in smaller bold italics or even just text italics.

The report will make most impact if it is brief and to the point. Read and re-read the draft to cut out any superfluous material or flabby writing.

> Look at any report you can get hold of – preferably one you have written yourself. How does it measure up to the precepts given above? How could it be improved?

MAKING PRESENTATIONS

The three keys to effective speaking are:

• thorough preparation

• good delivery

• overcoming nervousness.

Thorough preparation

Allow yourself ample time for preparation. You will probably need at least ten times as much as the actual duration of your talk. The main stages are:

1 *Get informed* – Collect and assemble all the facts and arguments you can get hold of.

2 *Decide what to say* – Define the main messages you want to get across. Limit the number to three or four – few people can absorb more than this number of new ideas at any one time. Select the facts, arguments and examples which support your message.

3 *Structure your talk* – It should have the classic beginning, middle and end.
   – Start thinking about the middle first, for that should contain your main messages and the supporting facts, arguments and illustrations.
   – Arrange your points so that a cumulative impact and a logical flow of ideas is achieved.
   – Then turn to the opening of your talk. Your objectives should be to create attention, arouse interest and inspire confidence. Give your audience a trailer to what you are going to say. Underline the objective of your presentation – what *they* will get out of it.
   – Finally, think about how you are going to close your talk. First and last impressions are very important. End on a high note.

4 *Think carefully about length* – Never talk for more than 40 minutes at a time: 20 or 30 minutes is better. Very few speakers can keep people's attention for long. An audience is usually very interested to begin with (unless

you make a mess of your opening) but interest declines steadily until people realise that you are approaching the end. Then they perk up. Hence the importance of your conclusion.

- To keep their attention throughout, give interim summaries which reinforce what you are saying, and above all, hammer home your key points at intervals throughout your talk.
- Continuity is equally important. You should build your argument progressively until you come to a positive and convincing conclusion. Provide signposts, interim summaries and bridging sections which lead your audience naturally from one point to the next.

5 *Prepare your notes* – In the first place write out your introductory and concluding remarks in full and set out in some detail the main text of your talk. It is not usually necessary to write everything down.

You should then boil down your text to the key headings to which you will refer in your talk. Your aim should be to avoid reading your speech if you possibly can because that can completely remove any life from what you have to say. So as not to be pinned down behind a lectern it is better to write your summarised points on lined index cards to which you can refer easily as you go along.

6 *Prepare and use visual aids* – Because your audience will only absorb one-third of what you say, if that, reinforce your message with visual aids. Appeal to more than one sense at a time. Powerpoint slides or overhead projector acetates provide good back-up, but don't overdo them, and keep them simple. Too many visual aids can be distracting (keep them down to 15 or so in a half-hour presentation) and too many words, or an over-elaborate presentation, will divert, bore and confuse your audience. As a rule of thumb, try not to put more than five or six bullet points on a slide. Each point should contain not more than six or seven words. Audiences dislike having to read a lot of small print on an over-busy slide. Use diagrams and charts wherever possible to break up the

flow of words and illustrate points. If you want the members of your audience to read something fairly elaborate, distribute the material as a handout and take them through it.

7 *Rehearse* – Rehearsal is vital. It instils confidence, helps you to get your timing right, and enables you to polish your opening and closing remarks and co-ordinate your talk and visual aids. Rehearse the talk to yourself several times and note how long each section takes. Get used to expanding on your notes without waffling. Practise giving your talk out loud – standing up, if that is the way you are going to present it. Some people like to tape record themselves but that can be off-putting. It is better to get someone to hear you and provide constructive criticism. It may be hard to take, but it could do you a world of good.

8 *Check arrangements in the room* – Ensure that your overhead or slide projector works and you know how to operate it. Check also on focus and visibility. Before you begin your talk, check that your notes and visual aids are in the right order and to hand.

Good delivery
To deliver a presentation effectively the following approaches are desirable.

- Talk audibly and check that you can be heard at the back. Your task is to *project* your voice. It's easier when there is a microphone, but even then you have to think about getting your words across.

- Vary the pace (not too fast, not too slow), pitch and emphasis of your delivery. Use pauses to make a point.

- Try to be conversational and as informal as the occasion requires (but not too casual).

- Give every indication that you truly believe in what you are saying: audiences respond well to enthusiasm.

- Avoid a stilted delivery. That is why you must not read

your talk. If you are your natural self, people are more likely to be on your side. They will forgive the occasional pause to find the right word.

• Light relief is a good thing but don't drag in irrelevant jokes or, indeed, make jokes at all if you are no good at telling them. You do not *have* to tell jokes.

• Use short words and sentences.

• Keep your eyes on the audience, moving from person to person to demonstrate that you are addressing them all, and also to gauge their reactions to what you are saying.

• If you can manage without elaborate notes (your slides or a few cards may be sufficient), come out from behind the desk or lectern and get close to your audience. It is generally advisable to stand up so that you can project what you say better, unless it is a smallish meeting round a table.

• Use hands for gesture and emphasis in moderation (but don't alternatively put them in your pockets).

• Don't fidget.

• Stand naturally and upright.

• You can move around the platform a little to add variety – you don't want to look as if you are clutching the lectern for much-needed support. But avoid pacing up and down like a caged tiger.

Overcoming nervousness
Some nervousness is a good thing. It makes you prepare, makes you think, and makes the adrenaline flow, thus raising performance. But excessive nervousness ruins your effectiveness and must be controlled.

The common reasons for excessive nervousness are: fear of failure, fear of looking foolish, fear of breakdown, a sense of inferiority, and dread of the isolation of the speaker. To overcome nervousness you should:

• *practise* – Take every opportunity you can get to speak

in public. The more you do it, the more confident you will become. Solicit constructive criticism and act on it.

- *know your subject* – Get the facts, examples and illustrations you need to put across.

- *know your audience* – Who is going to be there? What are they expecting to hear? What will they want to get out of listening to you?

- *know your objective* – Make sure that you know what you want to achieve. Visualise, if you can, the thoughtful departure afterwards of each member of your audience having learned something new which he or she is going to put to practical use.

- *prepare* – If you know that you have prepared carefully as suggested above you will be much more confident on the day.

- *rehearse* – This is an essential method of overcoming nervousness.

Seize any chance you can get to make presentations. The more practice you get, the better. Assuming you get your chance, how well did it turn out, with reference to the points made above?

SUMMARY

- Influencing techniques involve asserting, bridging, attracting, observing and listening. Powerful logical arguments need to be developed and deployed which take account of each other person's point of view, which persuade them that the proposal is beneficial, and which answer their objections.

- Reports are most likely to be effective if they have a clear and logical structure, use plain words to convey meaning and present the material in ways which enable people to grasp the point and follow the argument easily.

- Presentations are most likely to be effective if they are prepared and rehearsed thoroughly, are well-structured, are well-delivered and make use of visual aids.

REFERENCES

1 Gower E. *The Complete Plain Words*. Harmondsworth, Penguin Books, 1962.

5 Teamwork

Flatter, process-based organisations rely increasingly on good teamwork. Customer-focused businesses are forming teams to work together to provide a complete range of services to groups of customers. Manufacturing companies use group-technology techniques and production 'cells' in which technicians work as multiskilled members of a team. Managers have to work as members of teams as well as team leaders.

On completing this chapter, a reader will understand and be able to explain

- the essential nature of group behaviour

- how groups develop

- how teams function and fail to function

- how to work effectively as a member of a team

- how to lead and build teams

- how to overcome the problems of dysfunctional teams.

GROUP BEHAVIOUR

Organisations essentially consist of groups of people who work together. They may be formal groups or teams set up to achieve a defined purpose, or they may be informal groups set up to include people who have some affinity with one another. It could be said that formal groups satisfy the needs of the organisation whereas informal groups satisfy the needs of their members. These needs may not necessarily coincide. Managements generally like to take what is called a 'unitarist' view of organisations, which is the belief that everyone works together and has the same interests at heart. In practice, however, organisations are pluralist in nature –

there are different interest-groups whose needs and expectations are not necessarily in accord with those of the organisation's management.

The ways in which people work together are affected by the nature of the task, the technology they use, and the *culture* of the organisation – its values and norms: 'the way we do things around here'.

Groups need to carry out two major functions:

- *tasks* – initiation, information-seeking, decision-making, taking action, responding to demands or requests
- *maintenance* – encouraging, clarifying, summarising, standard-setting, working amicably and co-operatively together.

In the course of carrying out their tasks groups can develop feelings and beliefs about how they work and should work together. This 'ideology' affects the attitudes and actions of group members and the degree of satisfaction they get out of being part of their group. If the group ideology is strong, its members identify closely with it. This may be a good thing, but it can go too far. There is the phenomenon known as 'group-think' which can lead to irrational decisions and the inhibition of flexibility and independent judgement. Undue group pressures exerted by members on one another can do more harm than good.

> In what ways can groups work positively or negatively, and how can the negative aspects be overcome?

HOW GROUPS DEVELOP

Four stages of group development have been identified by Tuckman[1]:

1 *Forming* – when there is anxiety, dependence on the leader, and testing to find out the nature of the situation and the task, and what behaviour is acceptable

2 *Storming* – where there is conflict, emotional resistance to the demands of the task, resistance to control and even rebellion against the leader

3 *Norming* – when group cohesion is developed, norms emerge, mutual support and co-operation increase, and the group acquires a sense of identity

4 *Performing* – when interpersonal problems are resolved, roles are flexible and functional, there are constructive attempts to complete tasks, and energy is available for objective work.

Think of any group of which you are member or about which you know. Which one of these four stages is it at, and what is the evidence for it in the shape of how the group performs?

HOW TEAMS FUNCTION

The definition of a team

As defined by Katzenbach and Smith[2],

A team is a small number of people with complementary skills who are committed to a common purpose, performance goals and approach for which they hold themselves mutually accountable.

The characteristics of effective teams

The characteristics of teams, as described by Katzenbach and Smith, are:

• Teams are the basic units of performance for most organisations. They meld together the skills, experiences and insights of several people.

• Teamwork applies to the whole organisation as well as specific teams. It represents 'a set of values that encourage behaviours such as listening and responding co-operatively to points of view expressed by others, giving others the benefit of the doubt, providing support to those who need it, and recognising the interests and achievements of others'.

- Teams are created and energised by significant performance challenges.

- Teams outperform individuals acting alone or in large organisational groupings, especially when performance requires multiple skills, judgements and experiences.

- Teams are flexible and responsive to changing events and demands. They can adjust their approach to new information and challenges with greater speed, accuracy and effectiveness than can individuals caught in the web of larger organisational conventions.

- High-performance teams invest much time and effort exploring, shaping and agreeing on a purpose that belongs to them, both collectively and individually. They are characterised by a deep sense of commitment to their growth and success.

Dysfunctional teams

The specification set out above is somewhat idealistic. Teams do not always work like that. They can fail to function effectively in the following ways:

- The atmosphere can be strained and over-formalised.

- Either there is too much discussion which gets nowhere, or discussion is inhibited by dominant members of the team.

- Team members do not really understand what they are there to do or the objectives or standards they are expected to achieve.

- People don't listen to one another.

- Disagreements are frequent and often relate to personalities and differences of opinion rather than to a reasoned discussion of alternative points of view.

- Decisions are not made jointly by team members.

- There is evidence of open personal attacks or hidden personal animosities.

- People do not feel free to express their opinions.

- Individual team members opt out or are allowed to opt out, leaving the others to do the work.

- There is little flexibility in the way in which team members operate – people tend to use a limited range of skills or specific tasks; there is little evidence of multi-skilling.

- The team leader dominates the team; more attention is given to who takes control than to who is getting the work done.

- The team determines its own standards and norms, which may not be in accord with the standards and norms of the organisation.

> Do you know of any team which displays some or all of these characteristics? Why do you think it is like that?

Types of teams

There are many different types of teams in organisations. The main categories are:

- *organisational teams* – any fairly loose groupings in an organisation – for example, the top management team

- *work teams* – teams formed of people who are dependent on one another to deliver the specified results for which the team has been formed

- *project teams* – teams set up to plan and control a project which may carry on for months or even years

- *ad-hoc teams* – teams set up as taskforces or working parties to deal with specific issues.

> How would you classify any teams you know about using the above terms?

Team roles

The different types of roles played by team members have been defined by Belbin[3] as:

- *chairmen*, who control the way the team operates

- *shapers*, who specify the ways the team should work

- *company workers*, who turn proposals into practical work procedures

- *plants*, who produce ideas and strategies

- *resource investigators*, who explore the availability of resources, ideas and developments outside the team

- *monitor-evaluators*, who analyse problems and evaluate ideas

- *teamworkers*, who provide support to team members, improve team communications and foster team spirit

- *completer-finishers*, who maintain a sense of urgency in the team.

An alternative classification of roles has been developed by Margerison and McCann[4]. Their eight roles are:

- *reporter-advisor*, who gathers information and expresses it in an easily understandable form

- *creator-innovator*, who enjoys thinking up new ideas and ways of doing things

- *explorer-promoter*, who takes up ideas and promotes them to others

- *assessor-developer*, who takes ideas and makes them work in practice

- *thruster-organiser*, who gets things done, emphasising targets, deadlines and budgets

- *concluder-producer*, who sets up plans and standard systems to ensure outputs are achieved

- *controller-inspector*, who is concerned with the details and adhering to rules and regulations

- *upholder-maintainer*, who provides guidance and help in meeting standards.

According to Margerison and McCann, a balanced team needs members with preferences for each of these eight roles.

> Consider any team you are a member of or know. How balanced is it in terms of the Margerison–McCann roles?

HOW TO WORK EFFECTIVELY AS A MEMBER OF A TEAM

An effective team worker

- understands the part or parts he or she is expected to play as a member of the team

- is multiskilled – capable of carrying out a number of team-member roles

- is prepared to work flexibly

- takes a full part in team meetings and contributes useful ideas – is not afraid to express a point of view

- is tolerant and supportive of colleagues and respects other people's points of view

- works co-operatively with other members of the team.

> How would you rate yourself on a scale of 1 (poor) to 5 (excellent) as a team member under each of the above headings?

HOW TO BE AN EFFECTIVE TEAM LEADER

Competency requirements

Competencies can be developed specifically for team leaders, as in the following example of a differentiating competency definition (a differentiating competency distinguishes between high and low performers).

Definition

- guides, encourages and motivates teams to achieve the required result.

Positive indicators

- achieves high levels of performance from team
- defines objectives and plans clearly
- continually monitors performance and provides good feedback
- maintains effective relations with the team
- develops a sense of common purpose in the team
- builds team morale.

Negative indicators

- achieves poor team performance
- sets unclear objectives
- pays insufficient attention to team needs
- does not provide good feedback.

Achieving good teamwork

To achieve good teamwork, team leaders should

- establish urgency and direction
- as far as possible select members who have the required technical and teamworking skills
- pay particular attention to first meetings and actions
- agree team objectives and standards with the team
- assess people's performance not only on the results they achieve but on their capacity to work well in a team
- encourage team members to plan their own work, monitor control information and take action without reference to their team leader except in special circumstances (ie create a self-managed team)

- stimulate team members to come up with joint suggestions on how the performance of the team could be improved or working methods changed for the better (ie treat the team as an 'improvement group')

- hold special 'off-the-job' meetings regularly to discuss work-related issues, review progress and explore new ideas.

Review the above list of actions. Which do you think are the most important, and why?

You have just been appointed team leader. What are the first things you do?

Think of any team leader you know (including yourself, if appropriate). How well do they perform on a scale of 1 (poor) to 5 (excellent) under each of the above headings?

TEAM-BUILDING

Team-building activities can include helping people to learn about the interpersonal skills they need as teamworkers and exercising team leadership skills as described above. The process of team-building as a method of influencing attitudes and behaviour is illustrated in Figure 1.

If you are a team leader, you may be faced with a situation in which various forms of dysfunctional behaviour are being displayed. Training which covers the areas set out in Figure 1 can improve matters, but leadership by example is even more important. Team meetings can be held to explore and define helps and hindrances to effective working and to come to joint conclusions about what the team itself can do about it.

If, however, there are individual team members who are not contributing well, they may possibly lack the required skills or not be well motivated. They might therefore have to be dealt with specifically through a performance review process. This will include agreeing the standards of performance and competencies required by team members,

Figure 1 The process of team–building

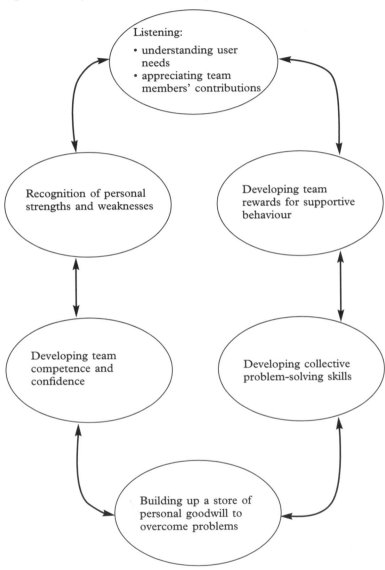

carrying out joint reviews of the behaviour of the individual with reference to actual examples, agreeing and implementing a personal development plan, giving positive feedback to recognise achievement and build on strengths, and providing encouragement, support, coaching and training as required.

Disruptive team members can be tackled in the same way, although their colleagues may exert some influence on them. If behaviour does not improve, consideration would have to be given to whether such individuals should be allowed to remain members of the team.

SUMMARY

- Organisations are composed of formal and informal groups.

- The ways in which groups function are affected by the nature of their task and the organisation's culture. Groups essentially have two functions: task and maintenance.

- Groups go through four development stages: forming, storming, norming and performing.

- Teams are the basic units of performance and can outperform individuals.

- Teams can be dysfunctional – groups may encounter conflict, disagreements and lack of consensus, and create for themselves norms in conflict with those of the organisation; individuals may be subject to oppression and allow themselves too little flexibility.

- The main types of teams are organisation teams, work teams, project teams and *ad-hoc* teams.

- Team members play a number of different roles.

- Effective team workers are multiskilled, prepared to work flexibly, play a full part in the team and work co-operatively with colleagues.

- To achieve good teamwork, team leaders must establish urgency and direction, select the right people, agree team objectives, assess the performance of individuals as teamworkers, encourage the development of self-managed teams, and hold regular meetings.

- Team-building activities can include various methods of influencing attitudes and behaviours, including performance reviews and training.

REFERENCES

1 TUCKMAN B. 'Developmental sequences in small groups', *Psychological Bulletin,* No. 63, 1965.

2 KATZENBACH J. *and* SMITH D. *The Magic of Teams.* Boston, Mass., Harvard Business School Press, 1993.

3 BELBIN M. *Management Teams: Why they succeed or fail.* London, Heinemann, 1981.

4 MARGERISON C. *and* MCCANN R. 'The Margerison–McCann team management resource theory and application', *International Journal of Manpower,* Vol. 7, No. 2, 1986; pp. 1–32.

6 Meetings

Meetings are an inevitable and often necessary part of a manager's job. A lot of time can be spent in them, and that time can easily be wasted. Cynics say that committees are made up of the unfit, appointed by the incompetent, to do the unnecessary – or that a camel is a horse designed by a committee. These comments may be gross exaggerations but many a manager at the end of a long day entirely filled with meetings feels that it has all been a waste of time and that the day could have been spent much more productively on 'real' work. There is a lot that needs to be done and that *can* be done to improve the effectiveness of meetings.

This chapter addresses these issues. On completing it, a reader will understand and be able to explain:

* the nature of meetings, working-parties and committees

* why and when meetings are necessary or unnecessary

* the criteria for a successful meeting

* how to set up a meeting

* how to chair a meeting

* the roles played by members of meetings

* how to be a member of a meeting.

THE NATURE OF MEETINGS, WORKING-PARTIES AND COMMITTEES

Meetings are gatherings of people convened to discuss a particular issue and reach a collective decision. Meetings may be *ad-hoc* to deal with a particular issue, or they may be held on a regular basis.

Working-parties are groups of people who are brought together to get something done – to deal with a problem, to discuss and plan an innovation, or to prepare for and oversee a project. They may also be called project teams or taskforces.

Committees are formally constituted bodies of people who meet regularly to discuss policy and planning issues, review performance and agree on actions in accordance with terms of reference.

The rest of this chapter is concerned mainly with meetings and committees, although the suggested approaches apply equally well to project teams and working-parties.

WHY AND WHEN MEETINGS SHOULD BE HELD

A meeting is a gathering of people with relevant expertise, experience and interests who contribute through discussion to the analysis of a situation and to a decision or recommendation on a course of action. The key point about meetings is that they exist for a purpose and their participant members should all be capable of contributing to the achievement of that purpose.

Why have meetings?
There are four assumptions usually made about why meetings are necessary.

1 They bring together people with different experience, roles and points of view. By taking account of all the considerations brought forward by this range of people (exchanging ideas) a solution will be produced which will be superior to one developed by any single person or number of people working independently. This is the principle of *synergy* – the whole is greater than the sum of the parts.

2 They ensure that the major interests in an issue or a problem are represented so that appropriate account can be taken of those interests when reaching a decision.

3 They provide a means for communicating views and information to interested parties.

4 They save time by assembling relevant people in one place at one time.

When to have meetings

The first two of the reasons given above may provide a sufficient justification for convening a meeting. But the use of a meeting as a vehicle for communication may not always be justified. There are other, more efficient, ways of communicating. And meetings can easily waste, rather than save, time.

It is too easy for people to believe that a meeting is the only way to sort something out. They say 'Let's get together and talk about it', without considering whether two or three brief conversations with interested people might suffice, and without deciding on the specific purpose of the meeting.

More meetings fail because the purpose has not been defined clearly enough than for any other reason. The end-result expected from a meeting – a decision, proposal or recommendation – should be spelled out so that people at the meeting know why they are there and understand what they are collectively expected to deliver.

CRITERIA FOR AN EFFECTIVE MEETING

An effective meeting is one that in as short a time as possible achieves consensus by listening to and assessing different viewpoints and then proposes a specific, relevant and practical course of action.

What can go wrong at meetings

But meetings do not always work as well as this. Things that can go wrong include:

- wasting time – too many people talk (waffle) too much

- failing to come up with a solution – meetings can be slow, exasperating and frustrating, and they can legitimise procrastination and indecisiveness (meetings are sometimes called by people as a means of putting off the taxing process of having to make an independent decision)

- being dominated by a few people with strong personalities

- making lowest-common-denominator decisions – ie decisions which represent an easy way out favoured by the majority of people attending the meeting

- encouraging political decisions reached where vested interests prevail by means of lobbying and pressure

- diluting responsibility.

Conducting an effective meeting

Putting these failures into reverse, an effective meeting is one in which

- people talk to the point (or are kept that way)

- decisions are made swiftly but after proper debate

- everyone with something to say contributes

- consensus is not achieved by going for the easiest or most generally acceptable solution

- discussions are open – there are no hidden agendas, the meeting is responsible for the decision, and that decision will not already have been taken behind closed doors (ie the meeting is not acting as a rubber stamp)

- no individual's authority is usurped – it will be for someone designated by the meeting to take action afterwards

- managers are not allowed to shift their individual responsibility to the assembly – if they are there to make decisions, then they should make them (this does not, of course, preclude them from talking to other people and networking)

- overall duration is restricted to no longer than two hours (one hour is better) – this may sound arbitrary but long meetings tend to encourage discursiveness and people lose interest because they are preoccupied with their 'real' work: 'What am I doing here?' they say to themselves

• issues are addressed which are within the members'
comprehension – if asked to agree to something big or
complex, members will in any case want to leave it to the
experts (so why raise it at the meeting?).

Northcote Parkinson, of Parkinson's Law fame, cited
committees which approved a £1-million capital project
(which they couldn't understand) in 10 minutes flat while
spending two hours wrangling over a £800 cycle-shed. What
point was he making?

SETTING UP A MEETING

There are six things to do when setting up a meeting.

1 Ask yourself: 'Is this meeting really necessary?' What
can be achieved by dragging all these busy people into a
room to talk away possibly for hours about something
which possibly does not really concern them and on
which they possibly have little or nothing to contribute?
One reason for irrelevant and waffly discussions is that
people at meetings often feel compelled to say
something, however inappropriate, to justify their
presence there at all.

2 If the answer to the first question is Yes (it *is* really
necessary), the second question is 'Why?' The purpose of
the meeting must be defined: 'This is the issue. This is
why it needs to be addressed. This is what the meeting
has to achieve in the shape of a decision or
recommendation.' It does not, of course, mean spelling
out what the decision or recommendation should *be*,
but it does mean indicating what it should *be about*. The
chair of the meeting must be in a position to say
something like: 'We are here to consider the following
issue ..¤. We have to make up our minds what to do
about it so that a firm recommendation can be made to
management.'

3 Decide who is going to chair the meeting. The qualities
you are looking for are: understanding of the issues

(without necessarily knowing the answers) and demonstrated skills as a chair (these skills are described in the next section of the chapter) with the likelihood of retaining the respect and trust of the members of the meeting.

4 Decide who should attend the meeting. You should consider people who have a strong interest in the main issue and who can make a contribution. You do not want too many – six to eight is probably the most you need – but actually, the fewer the better. A meeting of two or three people may well achieve more than a meeting of 10 or 12. But you must ensure that the really interested parties are represented or the outcome of the meeting may be regarded as a 'stitch-up'. The people you invite should be told what the meeting is about and why they have been asked to attend.

5 Draw up terms of reference (this is what the meeting is for) and an agenda (this is what we are going to talk about). Supporting papers can be attached to the agenda but they should be brief. People have better things to do than wade through reams of paper.

6 Finally, fix the time and place, inform people accordingly, and give them the agenda and supporting papers.

PREPARING FOR A MEETING

Chairing

If you are chairing a meeting, you should familiarise yourself with the issues in advance and ensure that you have absorbed the relevant information. You should try to avoid leaping to conclusions before the meeting – conclusions should come out of it; they should not be pre-judged. Think about who is going to be present and what they may contribute so that you can draw them out if they do not come forward with their views. Finally, study the agenda and very broadly allocate a duration for each item so that you can complete the meeting in good time. You cannot be precise about timings but it is useful to have some guidelines.

Acting as secretary

If you are acting as secretary to the meeting, ensure that everyone knows when and where it is to take place and who will be present. Get the agenda and supporting papers out in good time. Nothing irritates committee members more than being confronted with a heap of papers only 24 hours before the meeting. Ensure that the meeting room is adequate – enough space, quiet, reasonably comfortable chairs, good ventilation, visual aid equipment as required, refreshments as necessary. Take along spare agendas and supporting papers – someone always leaves theirs behind.

CHAIRING A MEETING

To chair a meeting effectively, you should:

1 Start by defining the purpose of the meeting, also setting a timescale which you intend to keep.

2 Go through each item on the agenda in turn, ensuring that consensus is achieved as far as possible, and that a firm conclusion on each is reached and recorded.

3 Initiate the discussion on each item by setting the scene and inviting contributions.

4 Allow no one person or clique to dominate the discussion.

5 Invite contributions from members of the meeting generally.

6 Bring people back to order if they drift from the point.

7 Where the discussion is going on too long or dragging, remind people that they are there to get something agreed, not just to talk – 'Let's make progress.'

8 Encourage the expression of different points of view.

9 Avoid crushing, and allow no one else to crush, a contribution even if it is not particularly relevant – 'That's an interesting point – are there any other views?'

10 Allow disagreement between members of the meeting

but step in smartly if the discussion becomes too contentious.

11 Chip in with questions or brief comments from time to time to clarify a point or help to make progress, but avoid dominating the discussion yourself.

12 At appropriate moments, summarise the discussion and express views on where the meeting has got to, especially if the meeting is straying from the point or getting bogged down.

13 If an interim or final conclusion appears to have been reached, outline your perception of what has been agreed. Next check that the meeting concurs with this summary, amending it as necessary. And finally, ensure that the decision is recorded and agreed exactly as made.

14 At the end of the meeting summarise what has been achieved, setting out action points for the record and indicating who is responsible for taking action, and when.

15 If a further meeting is required, agree the purpose of the meeting, when and where it is to take place, and what has to be done by those present before it happens.

Think about any meeting you have attended. How would you rate the chair (excellent, good, OK, not so good, poor) against the criteria listed above?

You are chairing a meeting. Two members get into an argument which appears to be degenerating into a slanging-match. What do you say to them?

You are chairing a meeting. You cannot get consensus on a decision. What do you do?

You are chairing a meeting. You disagree strongly with the conclusions that are emerging from the discussion. What do you do?

HOW TO BE AN EFFECTIVE MEMBER OF A MEETING

To be an effective member of a meeting, you should:

- Prepare thoroughly – have all the facts at your fingertips, with any supporting data you need.

- Make your points clearly, succinctly and positively – try to resist the temptation to talk too much.

- Remain silent if you have nothing to say – 'keep your powder dry' until you can make a worthwhile contribution.

- Listen, observe and save your arguments until you can make a really telling point; don't plunge in too quickly or effusively – there may be other compelling arguments.

- Avoid making such statements as 'I think we must do this' if you are not sure of your ground; instead, pose a question to the chair or other members of the meeting in such a form as 'Do you think there is a case for doing this?'

- Be prepared to argue your case firmly, but don't persist in fighting for a lost cause – don't retire in a sulk because you cannot get your own way: accept defeat gracefully.

- Remember that if you are defeated in committee there may still be a chance for you to fight another day in a different setting.

> Think about the last meeting you attended. How well did you measure up to the criteria set out above?

SUMMARY

- Meetings are gatherings of people who discuss and come to conclusions on particular issues. Working-parties are set up to tackle a problem or a project. Committees are groups of people who meet regularly to discuss policies and plans and come to decisions on actions.

- Meetings are held because they bring together different experiences and points of view to discuss and resolve an issue.

- An effective meeting reaches a firm conclusion based on the contributions of its members.

- Meetings need to be carefully planned.

- Chairing a meeting is a demanding role which requires considerable interpersonal skills in controlling and progressing discussions to reach a firm conclusion.

- Effectiveness at a meeting depends on preparation, clarity of expression, and taking part in discussions in a measured and careful way.

Part 2

THE WORK ENVIRONMENT

7 The principal functions in an organisation

Organisations exist to achieve an overall purpose, but achievement is only possible if the activities required to fulfil that purpose are identified and catered for. These activities are allocated to 'functions' which are concerned with particular aspects of the work of the organisation. Functions may be identified as distinct groups of activities, but it is essential to ensure that they operate in concert – that they are working together towards the same end, providing mutual support and co-operation and ensuring that multi-functional projects and cross-functional processes flow smoothly in the right direction. There is therefore an overarching function – that of general management – to ensure that corporate strategies and objectives are defined and understood, and that the work of the different functions is planned, organised, directed, co-ordinated and controlled to ensure that the goals of the business are achieved.

At the end of this chapter, a reader will understand and be able to explain:

• the role of general management in an organisation

• the role of such key functions in an organisation as research and development, marketing and sales, operations and production, purchasing, finance, information technology (IT) and personnel and development

• how the various functions interact

• how 'unity of purpose' can be achieved – ways in which the different functions can work effectively together and be developed.

THE ROLE OF GENERAL MANAGEMENT

General management is exercised by those in charge of an organisation – the chief executive – or those who are responsible for a group of functions in a strategic business unit, a manufacturing plant or a division. The role of general management is to plan, organise, direct, co-ordinate and control a number of interrelated functions, operations and services in order to achieve the organisation's mission and goals. General management is particularly concerned with:

• setting the direction – defining the mission of the organisation, developing strategic plans (strategic management) and clarifying goals

• defining core values

• providing visionary leadership

• taking action to transform the organisation as required

• directing, co-ordinating and controlling the various activities to ensure that objectives are achieved and core values upheld.

Mission statements

A *mission statement* sets out in broad terms why the organisation exists – what it is there to do and how it intends to do it. Mission statements provide the foundation upon which strategic plans and definitions of core values are built. They serve as a point of reference if the questions 'Why are we doing this?', 'Should we be doing this?' and 'How should we do this?' need to be answered. General management – in the shape of the chief executive supported by his or her top management team – is responsible for answering these questions.

Strategic management

Strategic management is a continuing process consisting of a sequence of activities: strategy formulation, strategic planning, implementation, review and updating. It requires general management to look ahead at what it wants the organisation to achieve in the middle or relatively distant future and answer three basic questions:

1 Where are we now?

2 Where do we want to be?

3 How are we going to get there?

Strategic management is concerned with both ends and means. For its ends it describes a vision of what the organisation will look like in a few years' time. For the means it shows how the vision will be realised. Strategic management is about defining intentions and ways of fulfilling these intentions. As Rosabeth Moss Kanter[1] writes: 'Strategic plans elicit the present actions for the future' and become 'action vehicles – integrating and institutionalising mechanisms for change'. She goes on to say:

> Strong leaders articulate direction and save the organisation from change by drift ... They see a vision of the future that allows them to see more clearly what steps to take, building on present capacities and strengths.

Objective-setting

A primary role of general managers is to define the challenge facing the organisation. This means setting objectives. As Drucker[2] wrote:

> Objectives are needed in every area where performance and results directly and vitally affect the management of the business. Objectives enable management to explain, predict, direct and control activities in ways in which a single idea like profit maximisation does not.

The key words in this statement about objectives are that they:

- *explain* – this, specifically, is what this organisation has to do: this is how it will attain its mission and meet the expectations of its stakeholders

- *predict* – this is what this organisation will achieve

- *direct* – these are the organisation's goals: this is where we intend to go

- *control* – these are the criteria against which we shall measure our performance and monitor our progress towards our goals.

Top management sets the overall objectives and ensures that they are supported by the objectives set at each level of the organisation. If, for example, one objective is to reduce the amount of working capital, management might set an overall target for increasing the stock turnover rate (the cost of sales divided by the value of stock). Managers who are stock (inventory) holders will be expected to set objectives for their stock turnover which will contribute to the achievement of the overall target. At the next level down, individual stock users will be expected to set and achieve targets for reducing the levels of inventory they hold without prejudicing customer service (there is a delicate balance between reducing stock levels and maintaining acceptable levels of customer service).

The aim is to integrate functional, team and individual objectives with the corporate objectives. This is sometimes described as a process of 'cascading' objectives down through the organisation. But enlightened managements appreciate that a top-down approach to prescribing objectives will not ensure that the individuals and teams concerned will own them – will 'buy into' them. They recognise that ownership of and therefore commitment to objectives is much more likely to happen if people can contribute to the process of setting objectives on a 'bottom-up' basis. Of course, the overriding objective or challenge remains, but at least teams and individuals have a say in what they believe they can realistically achieve.

Defining core values

Core values express beliefs in what is best or good for the organisation and what sort of behaviour is desirable. An organisation is said to be 'value-driven' when the 'value set' (the range of core values) is shared and acted upon throughout the business.

Values may be concerned with such aspects of organisational behaviour as care for customers, quality, teamwork, performance-orientation and social responsibility. They may be articulated by management, but it is not enough for them simply to be espoused at the top. They are much more likely to be accepted and implemented if management engages in a dialogue with people throughout the organisation to promote understanding and action in support of the values.

Providing visionary leadership

General managers should be able to 'envision' what the organisation should become and what it should achieve, and to ensure that their vision is realised. In the words of Tom Peters:[3]

> The vision, and managers' consistent, daily actions in support of it, is the sea anchor, the basis for keeping people from running around as the waves of change toss them to and fro.

Bill Richardson[4] suggests that visionary leaders are

- oriented towards action – they prefer to talk rather than to write or plan
- good communicators, capable of ensuring that the meaning and implications of their vision are shared throughout the organisation
- seekers of excellence – spotting mismatches between how things are done now and how they could be once improved
- people who form their visions by listening and observing; their new approaches are based on making connections between what is happening somewhere else and how it might be applied to their own areas
- calculated risk-takers.

Organisational transformation

General managers, especially those at the top of organisations, may be involved in programmes designed to transform the organisation. This may be a reaction to a crisis – loss of confidence by shareholders – and the appointment of a new chief executive to turn round the business. Or the existing top management may decide that the time has come to change radically what the organisation does, how it does it, the sort of people it employs, and the way it is organised.

Transformation programmes start by a definition at the top of what business the organisation is in and what business the organisation *ought* to be in. The next step is to define what needs to be done to get from A to B. Organisational transformation is therefore largely about change management, as discussed in Chapter 16.

Transformation programmes are very much the responsibility of general managers. They have to set the direction and ensure that the transitional activities (getting from here to there) drive the change. They have to demonstrate their active support for the change and their active involvement in the change process. Innovations arising from transformational programmes will not work without this drive and support.

Providing direction and control

General managers define strategic goals, but they also provide the overall direction to ensure that progress is made as planned. This means that they must monitor what is happening and initiate corrective action if things are going wrong.

Co-ordinating

General managers achieve 'unity of effort' by ensuring that activities are co-ordinated in order to achieve the planned result. Co-ordination is achieved by the processes of planning, organising, delegating, communicating and controlling, as discussed in Chapter 2 of this book.

> List and explain four characteristics of the role of a typical general manager.
> 'A leader shapes and shares a vision which gives point to the work of others' (Charles Handy[5]). What are the implications of this definition of a leader?
> What does 'cascading' objectives mean? What is the purpose of cascading? Does the concept create any problems, and if so, how may they be overcome?
> What is the most important thing that general managers do? Provide some examples from your own observations.

THE PRINCIPAL FUNCTIONS

The principal functions in organisations described in the rest of this chapter are research and development, marketing and sales, operations and production, purchasing, finance, information technology, and personnel and development. They are examined separately but it must be emphasised that they do not – cannot – exist in isolation. They are all interdependent. It should also be mentioned that there are, of course, wide variations in how these functions are practised in different organisations. The descriptions are generalised versions of the typical activities carried out within typical functions. There are a number of functions not mentioned here which exist in many organisations – for example, legal, property, management services (a term which sometimes embraces IT), facilities or office management, fund-raising (in charities), and public affairs.

RESEARCH AND DEVELOPMENT

The research and development (R&D) function designs and develops new products or services and modifies existing ones to create or satisfy customer needs and wants now and in the future.

R&D activities
The main R&D activities are:

• *basic research* – This is sometimes called 'blue skies'

research, in which scientists delve into such things as the basic properties of materials. Their aim will be to achieve breakthroughs in the discovery of new products and applications which can be developed for manufacture and sale. Basic research is carried out in such industries as pharmaceuticals, biotechnology, metal and glass processing and fabrication, electronics, IT and aerospace.

* *applied research* – This is either the application of one of basic research's discoveries to its possible use in manufacturing or the further development of a product or service. A structures engineer in an aerospace firm might for example apply the output of basic research into the properties of relevant material such as titanium to the design of an aircraft or missile.

* *development* – This takes a concept or idea that may have been generated by applied research and converts it into a process or product for use or sale.

* *design* – This works in conjunction with development, marketing and production to design the final process or product. Designers prepare specifications and use computer-aided design (CAD) processes. These provide a design-engineering database for manufacturing and are linked to computer-aided manufacturing (CAM) processes to produce a CADCAM system for the computer integration of such processes as computer numerical control (CNC).

MARKETING

Marketing is the management process which identifies, anticipates, influences and satisfies the wants and needs of customers profitably. According to Theodore Levitt[6], 'The purpose of a business is to get and keep a customer.'

Marketing defines target markets – the actual and potential buyers of a product or service – and decides how the wants and needs of people in these markets can be created and met more effectively and efficiently than competitors can create and meet them. Marketing seeks to achieve competitive advantage by providing value for customers – value that will be measured in such terms as the extent to which a need is met, the quality of the product or service, its cost, and the quality of after-sales service.

Levitt[7] sums up the marketing concept thus:

> The organisation must learn to think of itself not as producing goods or service but as *buying customers*, as doing the things that will make people *want* to do business with it.

Marketing activities

The main marketing activities are:

- *marketing planning* – This is the central marketing activity and involves the analysis of market opportunities, the selection of target markets, and the preparation of plans for market, product/service development. Marketing planning also involves the preparation of action plans for achieving sales targets.

- *product development* – The preparation and implementation of programmes for developing, testing and launching new products or services.

- *advertising* – The preparation of advertising campaigns. This includes media planning – deciding what media to use.

- *marketing research* – The complilation of information on the company's actual and potential markets and on existing and potential users of the products and services marketed by the company.

- *product market analysis* – Product analysis studies the product life-cycle (the sales pattern of the growth and decline of demand for a product over a period of time) to describe and forecast the pattern of sales for a product or service. Market analysis identifies gaps in the market (gap analysis) which are not filled by competitors' products and could be exploited by the company.

- *target marketing* – This defines the different groups that make up a market (segmentation) in order to make decisions on where marketing effort should be targeted.

- *developing the marketing mix* – The marketing mix is the set of controllable variables that the company blends to produce the response it wants in its target markets. The elements of the mix consist of product, price, place and promotion.

- *pricing* – This is the process of setting competitive but profitable price levels.

- *relationship marketing* – This is the process of building good customer relations.

- *database marketing* – This uses the company's database of information about customers and their buying habits to target sales to individual buyers.

What is the essential nature of the marketing concept?
What is meant by the terms 'product life-cycle', 'segmentation' and 'target marketing'?
Why is effective marketing effort fundamental to the continued success of a business?

SELLING: THE SALES FUNCTION

Selling is the process of persuading customers to buy and continue to buy the products or services of the business. The sales cycle consists of attracting customers, presenting the product to customers, convincing customers that this product is what they want, and completing the sale. Marketing identifies and defines the products and services customers will want to purchase, and sales ensures that they buy those goods or services.

Selling activities
The main selling activities are:

- *sales planning* – setting sales targets and deciding how they are going to be reached. In a direct sales operation this includes decisions on what sort of sales staff and how many of them are required, how they are to be deployed, and how their sales activities should be scheduled. In a mail-order operation this involves planning media and mailing campaigns to present buying opportunities to customers

- *direct sales operations* – deploying the sales force in the field, ensuring that they make contact with customers and generate sales

- *field sales control* – monitoring sales performance in the field against indicators for inputs (number of calls, the cost of sales) and outputs (sales revenue).

> What are the essential differences between marketing and sales?
> How would you measure the effectiveness of sales effort?

OPERATIONS MANAGEMENT

Operations management is concerned with the planning, direction and control of the fundamental activities which the organisation exists to carry out. These activities will be to make, provide or sell products or services.

In a profit-making company the aims of operations management are firstly to create added value for the organisation. Added value is the difference between the income of the business arising from sales and the amount spent on materials and other goods and services. Adding value means creating more out of less. Secondly, operations management in a profit-making business aims to achieve sustainable competitive advantage by satisfying the demands and needs of customers for the company's products. Competitive advantage is achieved by a firm's creating extra value for its customers and thus excelling in its markets compared with its competitors. Operations management can include production management as described in the next section. It can also cover distribution – storing products in the plant and distributing them to depots, wholesalers, retailers or direct to customers.

In not-for-profit organisations, including government departments, local authorities, government agencies and charities, the aim of operations management is to deliver cost-effective services which meet the requirements of the public or clients and achieve the target levels defined by performance indicators.

Operations management activities

The main operations management activities are:

* *planning* – deciding what goods to produce or services to provide (type, quality), programme timing, the methods to be used; determining the resources required to provide or deliver the goods or services; organising and allocating those resources; scheduling the production or delivery of services

* *production/delivery* – overseeing the manufacturing or service delivery processes to achieve targeted performance levels

* *control* – monitoring progress and performance to ensure that targets are achieved.

> Consider your own organisation or one with which you are familiar. What are the main operational management activities, and what results are they expected to achieve?

PRODUCTION MANAGEMENT

Production management involves the procurement, deployment and use of resources to manufacture products for distribution and sale to customers. It transforms inputs in the shape of raw materials and bought-in or subcontracted parts into outputs in the form of finished goods.

Transformation is achieved through people. But production management is concerned with devising the methods and techniques they use, procuring the materials they need, designing and developing the manufacturing systems and processes they operate, and providing them with the required plant, machinery, equipment and tools.

Production management is also very much concerned with exercising direction and control in order to achieve targets, standards and budgets for output, quality, timeliness (delivery on time) and cost.

Production management activities

The main production management activities are:

- *manufacturing systems* – the development and operation of manufacturing systems. These may consist of job, batch or flow production systems, the operation of computer-numerically-controlled machine-tools, computer-integrated manufacture, and the use of robots

- *production engineering* – the activities concerned with specifying, planning and controlling manufacturing processes. The main production engineering activities are process planning, production planning and production control, as described below

- *process planning* – determining how a product or part should be manufactured

- *production planning* – the analysis of sales forecasts and others in order to decide on the manufacturing resources (people, capacity and materials) required to meet current and anticipated demand

- *production control* – scheduling production, loading work onto machines, controlling the availability and use of materials, and assigning work to people

- *just-in-time* – enabling the right quantities of materials or parts to be made available and the right quantities to be produced at the right time

- *quality management* – applying quality control, quality assurance and total quality management systems

- *inventory control* – ensuring that the optimum amount of inventory or stock is held by the company so that its internal and external demand requirements are met economically

- *planned maintenance* – developing and implementing plant, equipment and building maintenance programmes to ensure that they operate or remain trouble-free for a predetermined period

- *distribution* – storing and despatching goods.

> What do you think are likely to be the characteristics of an efficient and effective manufacturing plant?

PURCHASING MANAGEMENT

Purchasing management – also known as supplies management, procurement or buying – obtains in the right quantities and at the right price the materials, plant, equipment and bought-in parts or assemblies required by the organisation.

Purchasing activities

The main purchasing activities are:

- *supply planning* – using material requirement planning techniques and sales forecasts to develop master purchasing schedules which are exploded into detailed schedules of what components and materials need to be obtained week by week, over the whole planning horizon

- materials management – the formulation and monitoring of policies and procedures for reducing purchasing costs, for make-or-buy decisions (ie whether to make a component within the firm or to buy it from outside), and for making-for-stock or making-for-customer-order decisions. It is also concerned with the co-ordination of common requirements in different parts of the company

- *quality assurance* – ensuring that the right quality of goods and materials is bought

- *purchasing procedures* – initiating orders, selecting suppliers, negotiating and agreeing contracts, and ensuring that deliveries are made on time

- *stock management* – maintaining records, re-ordering stock, and stocktaking.

> Why is an effective purchasing function crucial to the success of a manufacturing company?

FINANCIAL MANAGEMENT

Financial management is concerned with all aspects of the financial affairs of an organisation – financial planning, financial accounting (keeping the books and preparing financial reports and statements), management accounting (measuring and analysing financial performance), and managing cash flows.

Financial management activities

The main financial management activities are:

- *financial planning* – predicting future financial requirements and the amount of income that will be generated or made available as the basis for decision-making, strategic planning and plans for raising the finance required to support the business strategy

- *financial accounting* – recording all financial transactions, preparing balance sheets, profit-and-loss and value-added statements and cash flow forecasts, and handling depreciation and inflation accounting

- *financial analysis* – interpreting and explaining the performance of the business in terms of variance analysis, cost-volume-profit analysis, sales-mix analysis, risk analysis, cost-effectiveness analysis and cost-benefit analysis. The outcomes of financial analyses are used as guides to business planning and decision-making

- *management accounting* – accounting for and allocating

expenditures, allocating costs to products and processes, preparing and controlling cost budgets and generally dealing with overhead accounting. Activity-based costing techniques may be used to assign the cost of activities to products based on the products' demand for each activity

- *capital appraisal and budgeting* – selecting and planning capital investments based on estimates of the financial returns likely to be obtained from those investments. The techniques used include accounting rate of return, payback, and discounted cash flow.

> What contribution do you think an effective finance function can make to organisational success?

INFORMATION TECHNOLOGY (IT) MANAGEMENT

IT management is concerned with developing and operating systems for collecting, storing, processing and communicating information. This includes the specification and selection of hardware, the development of networks and the specification or development of software applications.

IT activities

The main IT activities are:

- *data management* – the collection, organisation and storage of the data required to manage the business, and the production of information in the form of reports or in response to enquiries

- *application development* – carrying out or commissioning systems analyses and programmed work to develop IT systems and software which will satisfy business/user needs, or buying and perhaps modifying software packages from software houses

- *application management* – ensuring that IT applications

work effectively and advising users on the systems and how they should be operated

• *application modification* – modifying applications to meet changing business or user needs.

Peter Drucker[8] wrote that 'The typical large business 20 years hence will have fewer than half the levels of management of its counterpart today, and no more than a third of the managers ... Businesses, especially large ones, have little choice but to become information-based.' To what extent has this prophecy come true to date?

What impact has IT made in your organisation (or one with which you are familiar) recently?

PERSONNEL AND DEVELOPMENT MANAGEMENT

Personnel and development management is concerned with the management and development of people in ways that contribute to the achievement of organisational effectiveness and meet their own needs for a satisfactory quality of working life, for security, and for the opportunity to use their abilities and develop their experience and skills.

The terms 'personnel and development' and 'human resource management' are often used interchangeably. Personnel managers have frequently had their job title changed to human resource managers without any discernible differences in how they carry out their roles.

On the other hand, human resource management (HRM) could be regarded as a different perspective – a new paradigm – for managing people in that there is more emphasis than in traditional approaches to personnel management on:

• adopting a strategic approach – one in which HR strategies are integrated with business strategies

• developing a more coherent approach to people-management processes concerned with resourcing, development and reward

- treating people as assets rather than costs – investing in them as a means of obtaining added value

- gaining the commitment of employees to the objectives and values of the organisation

- regarding people management as a line-management activity, not the preserve of the personnel function.

Personnel and development management activities

The main personnel and development activities are:

- *employee resourcing* – assessing future people requirements and planning to meet them (human resource planning); obtaining the number and type of people the organisation needs (recruitment and selection); dealing with redundancies, outplacement, dismissal and retirement (release from the organisation)

- *employee development* – systematically developing and implementing learning activities to enhance knowledge, skills and competencies and to increase the capacity of individuals to develop their careers and increase their employability; developing managers to ensure that the organisation has the effective managers it requires; planning and developing the careers of people with potential; generally developing organisational learning and creating a 'learning organisation'

- *organisational development* – planning and implementing programmes designed to improve organisational effectiveness and to help manage change; advising on organisational structures and job design

- *employee reward* – developing and administering reward systems which ensure that people are rewarded in accordance with their value to the organisation. The reward system consists of *processes* for measuring the internal and external value of jobs and the contribution of people in those jobs (job evaluation, market pricing and performance management), *practices* for motivating people by the use of financial and non-financial rewards, *structures* for relating pay and benefits to the value of the person to the organisation, and *schemes* for the provision of employee benefits

- *employee relations* – those activities carried out by management when it deals generally or collectively with individuals and their representatives or trade unions. Such activities consist of the management and maintenance of formal and informal relations with trade unions and their members (industrial relations); involving employees in decision-making on matters of mutual interest (involvement and participation); and creating and transmitting information of interest to employees (communications)

- *performance management* – obtaining better results from people and developing their capabilities by measuring and managing performance and creating personal development plans within agreed frameworks of objectives and competence requirements

- *health, safety and welfare services* – developing and administering health and safety programmes; providing welfare services; and helping with personal problems.

What contribution do you think an effective personnel department can make to organisational success?
How can this contribution be measured?
What do you think are the key qualities personnel practitioners should possess if they are to carry out their roles effectively?

SUMMARY

- The role of general management is to plan, organise, direct, co-ordinate and control a number of interrelated functions, operations and services in order to achieve the organisation's mission and goals.

- Research and development (R&D) designs and develops

new products or services and modifies existing ones to create or satisfy customer needs and wants now and in the future.

- Marketing is the management process which identifies, anticipates, influences and satisfies the wants and needs of customers profitably.

- Selling – the sales function – is the process of persuading customers to buy and continue to buy the products or services of the business.

- Operations management is concerned with the planning, direction and control of the fundamental activities which the organisation exists to carry out. These activities are to make, provide or sell products or services.

- Production management involves the procurement, deployment and use of resources to manufacture products for distribution and sale to customers. It transforms inputs in the shape of raw materials and bought-in or subcontracted parts into outputs in the form of finished goods.

- Purchasing management – also known as supplies management, procurement or buying – obtains in the right quantities and at the right price the materials, plant, equipment and bought-in parts or assemblies required by the organisation.

- Financial management is concerned with all aspects of the financial affairs of an organisation – financial planning, financial accounting (keeping the books and preparing financial reports and statements), management accounting (measuring and analysing financial performance) and managing cash flows.

- IT management is concerned with developing and operating systems for collecting, storing, processing and communicating information. This includes the specification and selection of hardware, the development of networks, and the specification or development of software applications.

- Personnel and development management is concerned with the management and development of people in ways that contribute to the achievement of organisational effectiveness and meet their own needs for a satisfactory quality of working life, for security, and for the opportunity to use their abilities and develop their experience and skills.

REFERENCES

1 KANTER R. M. *The Change Masters*. London, Allen & Unwin, 1984.

2 DRUCKER P. *The Practice of Management*. London, Heinemann, 1955.

3 PETERS T. *and* WATERMAN R. *In Search of Excellence*. New York, Harper & Row, 1982.

4 RICHARDSON W. 'The visionary leader', *Administrator*, September 1993; pp. 3–7.

5 HANDY C. *The Age of Unreason*. London, Business Books, 1989.

6 LEVITT T. 'Marketing myopia', *Harvard Business Review*, July–August 1960.

7 LEVITT, see Note 6 above.

8 DRUCKER P. 'The coming of the new organisation', *Harvard Business Review*, January–February 1988.

8 Organisational culture

The concept of organisational culture as described in this chapter is important to managers because it explains much of what happens in organisations and provides guidance on what can be done to improve organisational effectiveness.

On completing this chapter, a reader will be familiar with:

- the concepts of organisational culture and organisational climate

- the significance to organisations of the concept of culture and how a culture develops

- the components of a culture

- approaches to the analysis and description of organisational culture and climate

- methods of supporting or of changing culture.

DEFINITIONS

Organisational culture

Organisational or corporate culture is the pattern of values, norms, beliefs, attitudes and assumptions which may or may not have been articulated but which shape the ways people behave and things get done. *Values* refer to what is believed to be important about how people and the organisation should behave. *Norms* are the unwritten rules of behaviour.

This definition emphasises that organisational culture is concerned with abstractions such as values and norms which pervade the whole or part of an organisation. They may not be defined, discussed or even consciously noticed. Nevertheless, culture can have a significant influence on people's behaviour.

Organisational climate

Organisational climate refers to how people perceive (see and feel about) the culture existing in their organisation.

Management style

Management style describes the way in which individual managers set about achieving results through people. It is how managers behave as team leaders and how they exercise authority. Managers can be autocratic or democratic, tough or soft, demanding or easy-going, directive or *laissez-faire*, distant or accessible, destructive or supportive, task-oriented or people-oriented, rigid or flexible, considerate or unfeeling, friendly or cold, keyed up or relaxed. How they behave depends partly on themselves (their natural inclinations), partly on the example given to them by their managers, partly on the way in which they have been trained, and partly on organisational values and norms – accepted and typical ways of managerial behaviour.

THE SIGNIFICANCE OF CULTURE

The significance of culture is that it is rooted in deeply-held beliefs. It reflects what has functioned well in the past, embodying responses which have been accepted because they have met with success.

Culture can work for an organisation by creating an environment which is conducive to performance improvement and the management of change. It can work against an organisation by erecting barriers which prevent the attainment of corporate strategies. These barriers include resistance to change and lack of commitment.

The impact of culture can be to

* convey a sense of identity and unity of purpose to members of the organisation

* facilitate the generating of commitment and 'mutuality'

* shape behaviour by providing guidance on what is expected.

COMPONENTS OF ORGANISATIONAL CULTURE

Organisational culture can be described in terms of *values*, *norms* and *artefacts*. It will be perceived by members of the company in terms of the *organisational climate*, and it will influence, and be influenced by, the organisation's strategy, structure and systems.

Values

Values are beliefs in what is best or good for the organisation, and what should or ought to happen. The 'value set' of an organisation may only be recognised at top level, or it may be shared throughout the business, in which case the business may be described as 'value driven'.

The stronger the values, the more they influence behaviour. This does not depend upon their having been articulated. Implicit values which are deeply embedded in the culture of an organisation and are reinforced by the behaviour of management can be highly influential, whereas espoused values which are idealistic and are not reflected in managerial behaviour may have little or no effect.

Some of the areas in which values can most typically be expressed, implicitly or explicitly, are:

- performance
- competence
- competitiveness
- innovation
- quality
- customer service
- teamwork
- care and consideration for people.

Values are translated into reality through *norms* and *artefacts*, as described below. They may also be expressed through the media of language (organisational jargon), rituals, stories and myths.

Norms

Norms are the unwritten rules of behaviour, the 'rules of the game' which provide informal guidelines on how to behave. Norms tell people what they are supposed to be doing, saying, believing, even wearing. They are never expressed in writing – if they were, they would be policies or procedures. They are passed on by word of mouth or by example and can be enforced by the reactions of people if they are violated. They can exert very powerful pressure on behaviour because of these reactions – we control others by the way we react to them.

Norms correspond to such aspects of behaviour as

- how managers treat the members of their teams (management style) and how the team members relate to their managers

- the prevailing work ethic – eg 'work hard, play hard', 'come in early, stay late', 'if you cannot finish your work during business hours you are obviously inefficient', 'look busy at all times', 'look relaxed at all times'

- status – how much importance is attached to it; the existence or lack of obvious status symbols

- ambition – in some organisations naked ambition is expected and approved of; elsewhere a more subtle approach is the norm

- performance – exacting performance standards are general; the highest praise that can be given in some organisations is to be referred to as 'very professional'

- power – recognised as a way of life; executed by political means, dependent on expertise and ability rather than position; concentrated at the top; shared at different levels in different parts of the organisation

- politics – rife throughout the organisation and treated as normal behaviour; not accepted as overt behaviour

- loyalty – expected, a cradle-to-grave approach to careers; discounted, the emphasis is on results and contribution in the short term

- anger – may be openly expressed; may be hidden, but expressed through other, possibly political, means

- approachability – managers are mostly expected to be approachable and visible; otherwise, everything happens behind closed doors

- formality – a cool, formal approach is the norm; forenames may or may not be used at all levels; there are unwritten but clearly understood rules about dress.

Artefacts

Artefacts are the visible and tangible aspects of an organisation which people hear, see or feel. Artefacts can include such things as the working environment, the tone and language used in letters or memoranda, the manner in which people address each other at meetings or over the telephone, the welcome (or lack of welcome) given to visitors, and the way in which telephonists deal with outside calls.

HOW ORGANISATIONAL CULTURE DEVELOPS

The values and norms which are the basis of culture are formed in four ways. First, they are formed by the leaders in the organisation, especially those who have shaped them in the past. People identify with visionary leaders – how they behave and what they expect. They note what such leaders pay attention to and treat them as role models. Second, culture is formed around critical incidents – important events from which lessons are learned about desirable or undesirable behaviour. Third, culture develops from the need to maintain effective working relationships among organisation members, and this establishes values and expectations. Finally, culture is influenced by the organisation's environment. To a greater or lesser degree, the external environment may be dynamic, even turbulent, or it may be unchanging.

Culture is learned over a period of time. Where a culture has developed over long periods of time and has become firmly embedded it may be difficult to change quickly, if at all, unless a traumatic event occurs.

THE DIVERSITY OF CULTURE

The development process described above may result in a culture which characterises the whole organisation. But there may be different cultures within organisations. For example, the culture of an outward-looking marketing department may be substantially different from that of an internally-focused manufacturing function. There may be some common organisational values or norms, but in some respects cultures will differ between areas working in different environments.

CLASSIFYING ORGANISATIONAL CULTURE

There have been many attempts to develop culture typologies which can be used to analyse cultures as a basis for taking action to support or change them. Two of the best-known ones are Harrison's and Handy's.

Harrison[1] categorised what he called 'organisation ideologies'. These are:

- *power-oriented* – competitive, responsive to personality rather than expertise

- *people-oriented* – consensual, rejecting management control

- *task-oriented* – with a focus on competency, dynamic

- *role-oriented* – with a focus on legality, legitimacy and bureaucracy.

Handy[2] based his typology on Harrison's classification, although Handy prefers the word 'culture' to 'ideology' because 'culture' conveys more of the feeling of a pervasive way of life or set of norms. His four types of culture are:

- *the power culture* – one with a central power source which exercises control. There are few rules or procedures and the atmosphere is competitive, power-oriented and political

- *the role culture* – in which work is controlled by procedures and rules and the role, or job description, is more important than the person who fills it. Power is associated with positions, not people

- *the task culture* – in which the aim is to bring together the right people and let them get on with it. Influence is based more on expert power than on position or personal power. The culture is adaptable and teamwork is important

- *the person culture* – in which the individual is the central point. The organisation exists only to serve and assist the individuals in it.

In addition to referring to the typologies above, it is common practice to summarise the overriding characteristics of an organisation's culture in such terms as:

- *value-driven* – when the value set is put into practice as a way of life (operationalised)

- *customer-focused* – when the emphasis is on providing value to customers and customer-care programmes (see Chapter 15)

- *service-oriented* – when the focus is on service delivery and improving levels of service to customers or clients

- *high-performance* – when the focus is on achieving and sustaining high levels of performance in terms of profitability, output, productivity, innovation and quality: this might be expressed in the form of continuous improvement policies and processes (see Chapter 14)

- *high-involvement* – when management puts into practice involvement programmes which genuinely provide for employees to take part in decision-making processes on matters that affect them.

ASSESSING ORGANISATIONAL CULTURE

A number of instruments exist for assessing organisational culture. Assessment is not easy, because culture is concerned with both subjective beliefs and unconscious assumptions (which might be difficult to measure) and with observed phenomena such as behavioural norms and artefacts. One of the better-known instruments was developed by Harrison.[3] His questionnaire deals with the four orientations referred to earlier (power, role, task, self) and is completed by ranking statements according to what the respondent deems closest to the organisation's actual position. For example:

- A good boss is strong, decisive and firm but fair.

- A good subordinate is compliant, hard-working and loyal.

- People who do well in the organisation are shrewd and competitive, with a strong need for power.

- The basis of task assignment is the personal needs and judgements of those in authority.

- Decisions are made by people with the most knowledge and expertise about each problem.

MEASURING ORGANISATIONAL CLIMATE

Organisational-climate measures attempt to assess organisations in terms of those dimensions that are thought to capture or describe perceptions of the organisation, its general operation and its culture. One of the best-known instruments was devised by Litwin and Stringer[4] and takes account of the following specific dimensions:

- *structure* – feelings about constraints and freedom to act and the degree of formality or informality in the working atmosphere

- *responsibility* – the feeling of being trusted to carry out important work

- *risk* – the sense of riskiness and challenge in the job and in the organisation; the relative emphasis on taking calculated risks or playing it safe

- *warmth* – the existence of friendly and informal social groups

- *support* – the perceived helpfulness (or lack of it) of managers and co-workers; the emphasis (or lack of it) on mutual support

- *standards* – the perceived importance of implicit and explicit goals and performance standards; the emphasis on doing a good job; the challenge represented in personal and team goals

- *conflict* – the feeling that managers and other workers want to hear different opinions; the emphasis on getting problems out into the open rather than smoothing them over or ignoring them

- *identity* – the feeling that you belong to a company, that you are a valuable member of a working team.

APPROPRIATE CULTURES

It can be argued that a 'good' culture exerts a positive influence on organisational behaviour. It could help to create a 'high-performance' culture, one that will consistently produce a high level of business performance. As described by Furnham and Gunter,[5] 'A good culture is consistent in its components and shared amongst organisational members, and it makes the organisation unique, thus differentiating it from other organisations.'

Nonetheless, a high-performance culture corresponds to little more than any culture that produces a high level of business performance. The attributes of cultures vary tremendously by context. The qualities of a high-performance culture for an established retail chain, a growing service business and a consumer products company that is losing market share may be very different. Further: in addition to context differences, all cultures evolve over time. Cultures which are 'good' in one set of circumstances or period of time may be dysfunctional in different circumstances or at different times.

Because the culture is developed and manifests itself in different ways in different organisations, it is not possible to say that one culture is better than another, only that it is dissimilar in certain ways. There is no such thing as an ideal culture, only an appropriate culture. This means that there can be no universal prescription for managing culture – although there are certain approaches which can be helpful, as described in the next section.

SUPPORTING AND CHANGING CULTURES

It may not be possible to define an ideal structure or to prescribe how it can be developed, but it is certain that embedded cultures exert considerable influence on organisational behaviour and therefore performance. If there *is* an appropriate and effective culture, it would be desirable to take steps to support or reinforce it. If the culture is inappropriate, attempts should be made to determine what needs to be changed and to develop and implement plans for change.

Culture analysis

In either case, the first step is to analyse the existing culture. This can be done through questionnaires, surveys and discussions in focus groups or workshops. It is often helpful to involve people of an organisation in analysing the outcome of surveys, getting them to produce a diagnosis of the cultural issues facing the organisation and to participate in the development and implementation of plans and programmes to deal with pertinent issues.

Culture support and reinforcement

Culture support and reinforcement programmes aim to preserve and underpin what is good and functional about the currrent culture by

• reaffirming existing values through discussions and communications

- ensuring that values are put into practice (operationalising them)

- using the core values defined for the organisation (the value set) as headings for reviewing individual and team performance – emphasising that people are expected to uphold the values

- ensuring that induction procedures cover core values and how people are expected to achieve them

- reinforcing induction training with further training courses set up as part of a continuous development programme.

Culture change

In normal circumstances, cultural change programmes tend to focus on one or two particular areas which it is felt need to be given priority. Such programmes rarely, if ever, try to cover every aspect of organisational culture. The areas might, for example, be performance, commitment, quality, customer service or teamwork. In each case the underpinning values have to be defined. It would probably be necessary to prioritise by deciding which areas need the most urgent attention. There is a limit to how much can be done at once. The effectiveness of culture change programmes largely depends on the quality of change management processes, as described in Chapter 16.

Levers for change

Having identified what needs to be done, and the priorities, the next step is to consider what levers for change exist and how they can be used. The levers might or might not include:

- *performance* – performance-related or competence-related pay schemes; performance-management processes; gainsharing; leadership training, skills development

- *commitment* – communication, participation and involvement programmes; developing a climate of co-operation and trust; clarifying the psychological contract

- *quality* – total quality programmes

- *customer service* – customer-care programmes

- *teamwork* – team-building; team performance management; team rewards

- *values* – gaining understanding, acceptance and commitment through involvement in defining values, performance-management processes and employee-development interventions.

What difficulties might be met in attempting to change a culture? How could they be overcome?

Why is the concept of organisational culture significant to managers?

How can managers get a better understanding of their organisation's culture?

What do you think would be the characteristics of an organisation with a 'high-performance' culture?

What can be done to develop such a culture?

SUMMARY

- Organisational culture consists of the beliefs, values, attitudes, ways of behaving and assumptions which pervade an organisation and strongly influence how the organisation functions.

- The concept is important because it can make a significant impact on the effectiveness of the organisation and because anything that is done to introduce change must take it into account.

- Culture support and reinforcement programmes aim to preserve and underpin what is good and functional about the current culture by reaffirming and operationalising values.

- Culture change programmes aim to develop more appropriate cultures by the application of 'levers for change' performance-management and performance pay systems and total quality and customer-care processes.

REFERENCES

1 HARRISON R. 'Understanding your organization's character', *Harvard Business Review*, 5, 1972; pp. 119–128.

2 HANDY C. *Understanding Organisations*. Harmondsworth, Penguin Books, 1981.

3 HARRISON, see Note 1 above.

4 LITWIN G. H. *and* STRINGER R. A. *Motivation and Organisational Climate*. Boston, Mass., Harvard University Press, 1968.

5 FURNHAM A. *and* GUNTER B. *Corporate Assessment*. Routledge & Kegan Paul, London, 1993.

9 Organisation structure, design and development

On completing this chapter, a reader will understand and be able to explain:

- the meaning of the terms 'organisation', 'organisation structure', 'organisation design' and 'organisation development'

- how organisations function, including the need for specialisation and autonomy

- the different types of organisation structure – formal, informal, unitary, divisionalised, centralised, decentralised, matrix, process

- the concepts of the flexible firm, the core-periphery organisation and the '*ad hoc*-racy'

- the considerations affecting organisation and job/role design

- how to construct an organisation chart and write a job description or role definition

- approaches to organisation development.

DEFINITION OF TERMS

Organisation
Organisations get results by designing, developing and maintaining a system of co-ordinated activities in which individuals and groups of people work co-operatively under leadership towards commonly understood and accepted goals.

Organisation structures
Organisation structures are the framework for getting work done. They define and clarify

- how the activities required are grouped together into units, functions and departments

- who is responsible for what

- who reports to whom

- the lines of authority emanating from the top of the organisation.

Organisation design

The design of the structure is contingent upon the type of organisation, the activities carried out, the organisational culture (as described in Chapter 8) and the views or whims of those in charge. In traditional theory, organisation design is not affected by the characteristics of the members of the organisation. In practice, and increasingly so in these days of 'the flexible firm', organisation structures are adjusted or flexed in response to the type of people who are available or can be obtained to carry out the work.

Organisation charts

Organisation charts are used to illustrate the structure, but they can never represent the reality of how organisations operate – the cross-functional interactions and the different ways in which people work together. Job descriptions are used to define what is done – but again, they cannot convey the full flavour of the work carried out. If they do attempt to describe it in detail they defeat their own purpose through over-elaboration and by attempting to capture what is commonly an evolving role rather than a static set of duties.

Organisational development

Organisational development activities aim to improve the effectiveness of the organisation as a place where work gets done. They constitute the dynamic aspect of organising – breathing life into the structure.

HOW ORGANISATIONS FUNCTION

Organisations can be regarded as systems which exist in ever-changing and turbulent environments. As systems, they transform inputs (human, financial and physical resources) into outputs (goods and services).

An organisation has been described by Trist *et al*[1] as a 'socio-technical' system in which social processes (interactions between people) are interrelated with the technologies and operational methods used in the organisation.

In describing what goes on in organisations, the term *process* is frequently used today. 'Process' refers to *how* things get done, not *what* gets done. It embraces such aspects of organisational behaviour as leading, motivating, networking, working in teams, and planning and co-ordinating activities. Structures and systems are ways of helping to make 'process' work. There are a number of different views about how organisations function, as discussed below. But there is consensus on the fact that all organisations are concerned with specialisation and autonomy.

Traditional views on how organisations function

The classic or scientific management school as represented by Fayol,[2] Taylor[3] and Urwick[4] believed in order, control and formality. It was thought that organisations should minimise the opportunity for uncontrollable, and therefore unfortunate, informal relations, leaving room only for the formal ones. The term 'bureaucracy' was coined by Max Weber[5] to describe the type of organisation in which impersonality and rationality are developed to the highest degree. The ideal bureaucracy, according to Weber, has characteristic features:

- close job definition concerning duties and boundaries

- vertical authority patterns

- decisions based on expert judgement

- disciplined compliance with the directives of superiors

- maximum use of rules

- impersonal administration of staff.

The traditional approach to organisation emphasised formality – informality was not allowed. It was largely based on the military model such that a distinction was made between the line and the staff who both had rigidly-defined functions – the line did the fighting and the staff planned and provided support. The line-and-staff organisation became the model formal structure – the line exercises delegated authority to perform the functions of the enterprise and the staff organisation offers advice and provides the services required by the line organisation.

Recent views on how organisations function

The rebellion against the rigidities of the classic school was led by the contingency school (the best-known of whom were Burns and Stalker,[6] Woodward[7] and Lawrence and Lorsch[8]). Their overriding theme is that organisations are a function of the circumstances in which they exist. They oppose those who impose rigid principles of organisation irrespective of the technology or environmental conditions.

Pascale[9] believes that the new organisational paradigm should be regarded as having changed

• *from* the image of organisations as machines, with the emphasis on concrete strategy, structure and systems, *to* the idea of organisations as organisms, with the emphasis on the 'soft' dimensions of style and shared values

• *from* a hierarchical model, with step-by-step problem-solving, *to* a network model with parallel nodes of intelligence which surround problems until they are eliminated

• *from* the status-driven view that managers think, and workers do as they are told, *to* a view of managers as 'facilitators', with workers empowered to initiate improvements and change

• *from* an emphasis on 'vertical tasks' within functional units, *to* an emphasis on 'horizontal' tasks and collaboration across units

• *from* a focus on 'content' and the prescribed use of specific tools and techniques *to* a focus on 'process' and a holistic synthesis of techniques

• *from* the military model *to* a commitment model.

Specialisation

Organising is about getting teams and individuals to work collectively together to achieve a common purpose. But this involves a number of specialised activities which have to be catered for. For example, marketing is a general activity but within it there are specialisms such as market research. Production management requires specialists in computer-controlled manufacturing systems. Personnel management may need a specialist in employee reward (pay and benefits or compensation and benefits) systems.

These specialisms need to be identified and the expertise required obtained and developed to enable the practitioners to contribute in their particular field to achieving the collective effort. This raises an organisational problem: how can specialists, who may well be individualists, be made to fit into a team? How can the specialist contribution be consolidated into the overall effort?

The answer to both these questions is to ensure that from the very start the purpose of the specialist activity is identified as being part of the whole. The role it is expected to play has to be specified precisely. The contribution that the specialist is expected to make to the team should be clarified, and the need to integrate specialist with generalist activities must be addressed. Specialists can often make their best contribution if it is established that they are members of multi-disciplinary or multi-functional teams in which the part they play is defined.

> Can you think of three ways in which the work of specialists might be integrated with other activities?

Autonomy

According to the *Oxford English Dictionary* 'autonomy'

means the right of self-government and personal freedom. In organisations it means being given devolved authority and freedom to act without reference to another person, although such authority and freedom are constrained to some degree by the organisation's policies and core values and by external legislation and the expectations of stakeholders.

Enabling people to act autonomously within reasonable limits is desirable because:

• it means that decisions can be taken at the point of action by people who are 'close to the customer' or aware of the particular circumstances in which a decision has to be made

• it speeds up action and response time

• it empowers people, giving them greater job satisfaction – they are in control of their own actions and their work becomes meaningful because they can influence how it is done as well as what is done

• it focuses the attention of people on their responsibilities – it is more difficult for them to say that a complication is someone else's problem or that 'it's not in my job description'

• it is a means of developing initiative, a sense of responsibility and increased expertise.

But there are limits to autonomy. People have to conform to corporate policies and uphold core values. And, importantly, they have to work as members of teams, which may mean sacrificing a certain measure of individual autonomy for the good of the team.

Teams can be given a degree of autonomy as well as individuals. Self-managing teams (autonomous work groups) can be set up which may be largely self-regulating and work without close supervision. Such teams can be given the authority to plan, monitor and control their own work as long as they meet the targets and standards they have agreed.

Finally, autonomy can be given to strategic business units in a decentralised organisation. This autonomy may be governed by the requirement to deliver results, although *how* they deliver results is up to them.

What steps does an organisation need to take if it wants to increase the amount of autonomy given to a work team – for example, a team that provides services to groups of customers? Charles Handy[10] writes: 'One sign of the new sorts of organisation is a perceptible change in the language we use to talk about them. Organisations used to be perceived as gigantic pieces of engineering, with largely interchangeable parts ... Today the language is not that of engineering but of politics, with talk of cultures and networks, of teams and coalitions, of influence or power rather than control, of leadership not management.' To what extent is this happening or has it happened in your organisation, or one you know, and with what effect?

What lessons can be learned from the contemporary school of writers on organisation about approaches to organisation design?

FORMAL AND INFORMAL ORGANISATION

The formal organisation may be defined as a structure and described by means of an organisation chart. But that is not how it works. Some time ago, Chester Barnard[11] emphasised the importance of the informal organisation – the network of informal roles and relationships which, for better or worse, strongly influences the way formal structures operate. He wrote: 'Formal organisations come out of and are necessary to informal organisation: but when formal organisations come into operation, they create and require informal organisations.' Barnard's views were influenced by the so-called 'Hawthorne experiment', a large-scale investigation of productivity and industrial relations which took place at Western Electric's Hawthorne plant in the late 1920s and early 1930s. This highlighted the importance of informal groups and how they affected the way work was carried out.

More recently, Child[12] has pointed out that it is misleading to talk about a clear distinction between formal and informal organisation. Formality and informality can be built into the structure. And Burns and Stalker[13] have criticised the view that formal and informal organisation are mutually opposed social systems as described in 'the Manichean world of the Hawthorne studies'. It is perhaps better to make a distinction between the rigidly-defined 'line-and-staff' organisation, loved by the scientific management school, and the more flexible organisation of today, where it is recognised that process and interactions between people make them work, and that the lines on an organisation chart do not describe what really goes on. As Child has said, informality can be built into the structure if it is recognised that the structure need not be rigid. The 'process' organisation described later in this chapter illustrates how organisation design can cope with both the formal and the informal elements in one structure.

> What sort of informal processes can take place within a formal organisation structure?
> Consider your own organisation or one with which you are familiar: to what extent and where do informal processes influence the ways things get done?

TYPES OF ORGANISATION STRUCTURE

Unitary structure

A unitary structure is one that is found in self-contained organisations (those without divisions or subsidiaries) or in the separate units of divisionalised or decentralised organisations. In a unitary structure the heads of each function or department report directly to the top, as illustrated in Figure 2.

A unitary structure is the most basic type of organisation. It has the obvious advantage of clearly defining relationships – everyone knows where they are and a distinction is made between the line (production and sales) and staff (finance and personnel). The disadvantage of

Figure 2 A unitary organisation structure

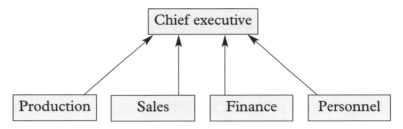

such a structure is that the departments might operate as separate 'organisational chimneys' – pursuing their ends without considering corporate needs and erecting boundaries between each other. Much depends on the capacity of the chief executive as a leader and team-builder to hold the organisation together.

Centralised structure

A centralised structure is one in which divisions, subsidiaries and geographically separated activities are subject to close control from the centre, which dictates what products they make or services they provide and how they should operate, and severely limits the extent to which independent decisions can be made locally.

A centralised structure is illustrated in Figure 3.

Figure 3 A centralised organisation structure

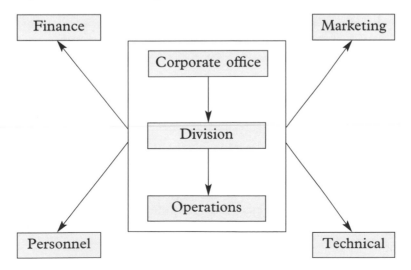

Advantages and disadvantages of centralisation
The advantages of centralisation are that

- control can be exercised over divisional activities to ensure that they are complying with group policy

- well-tried and tested products and services can be offered in standard packages to customers supported by country- or world-wide marketing and advertising campaigns, thus establishing a global brand image

- standard procedures and systems can be used without the need to develop new ones at local level – group resources can readily be made available to each division

- highly qualified and expert staff are available at headquarters to spell out to divisions how they can perform effectively.

The disadvantages of centralisation are that

- it constrains the ability of local management to determine what is best for their part of the business in the light of their understanding of their product, market or local circumstances

- it implies, incorrectly, that there is one best way to manage business affairs

- it restricts local enterprise and initiative to respond rapidly to new challenges and opportunities – the heavy hand of the centre is imposed on those in the business front line

- it creates double and unnecessary tiers of functional specialists and, often, an overstaffed and expensive headquarters.

Decentralised organisations

Some organisations, especially conglomerates, decentralise their manufacturing or service delivery activities to subsidiaries or strategic business units (SBUs). Only a few specialists remain at headquarters to deal with financial, taxation and legal matters. Personnel issues concerning senior management (recruitment, transfer, development and remuneration) may sometimes – but not always – be catered for at the centre.

The essence of decentralisation is that authority is delegated almost completely to the chief executives of the strategic business units to operate in their particular markets, so long as they meet profit and performance targets.

The research carried out by Goold and Campbell[14] established that there are three ways in which the centre can relate to its businesses:

• *strategic planning* – the centre develops strategy with the business units and sets broad, strategic performance targets.

• *financial control* – the centre exercises control through financial budgeting processes and by measuring performance in relation to profit targets; planning influence is low.

• *strategic control* – the centre leaves the units to develop their strategic plans but exercises tight control against strategic targets.

A decentralised organisation is illustrated in Figure 4.

Figure 4 A decentralised organisation structure

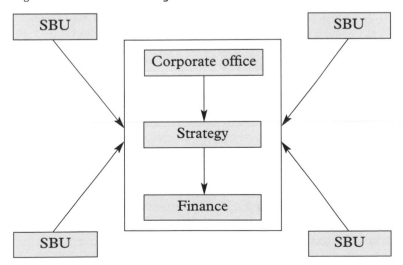

Advantages and disadvantages of decentralisation
The advantages of decentralisation are that:

- authority is given to the management of strategic business units to develop their products and markets

- the strategic business units can operate closely with their customers and respond quickly to product/market opportunities

- the cost of the central operation is minimised.

The disadvantages of decentralisation are that:

- business unit managements do not receive much support, if any, from the centre

- the scope for strategic business units to work together to exploit joint markets is severely limited – the tendency will in fact be for them to compete against each other

- the best use may not be made of the organisation's human and financial resources across the strategic business units – for example, career development for executives may be limited to their unit although both they and the organisation would benefit from planned career moves to other parts of the organisation.

Divisionalised organisations

The process of divisionalising organisations, as first described by Sloan[15] on the basis of his experience in running General Motors, involves structuring the organisation into separate divisions. Each division is concerned with discrete manufacturing, sales, distribution or service functions, or with serving a particular market. At group headquarters, functional departments are created in such areas as finance, planning, engineering, personnel and legal to provide services to the divisions. Importantly, they may exercise functional control over the activities of divisions in their area. Thus personnel may lay down that a standard job evaluation system has to be applied in each division, and finance may stipulate how budgets are to be prepared and submitted to headquarters. The amount of

Figure 5   A divisionalised organisation structure

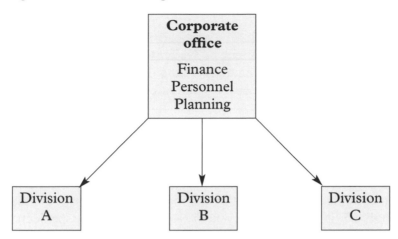

control exercised depends on the extent to which the organisation has decided to decentralise authority to divisions. Divisionalised organisations may appear to operate the same sort of structure as decentralised organisations but they treat each operational unit as a Strategic Business Unit. The form a divisionalised organisation may take is illustrated in Figure 5.

Advantages and disadvantages of divisionalised organisations

The advantages of a divisionalised organisation are that

- areas of responsibility can be clearly defined

- each division can be set up to carry out a discrete or closely linked set of activities

- functional services and control can be provided and exercised from the top so that a uniform approach to managing activities can be adopted.

The disadvantages are that

- individual divisions, as the word implies, can go their own way without reference to what is happening in the other divisions of the organisation

- concerted efforts to develop and exploit particular markets may be prejudiced

- the functional control exercised from the centre may inhibit the development of systems and processes which are appropriate to the markets the divisions serve and the environment in which they operate.

Matrix organisations

Matrix organisations carry out projects in such fields as contracting, research and development, and consultancy. Staff from various disciplines – for example, electrical and mechanical engineering in a contracting firm, or finance and IT in a consultancy firm – are assigned to projects. When a project is set up, a project leader is appointed and draws staff from the appropriate disciplines. Project-leading may be a full-time occupation or leaders may be senior specialists from the key project disciplines. While working on the project, team members are responsible to the team leader for the project work they do, but the functional head of the discipline has a general responsibility for ensuring that proper standards are maintained by discipline members. The members continue to be functionally responsible to the head of the discipline, and when a project ends they return to the discipline until they are assigned to a new project. The head of the discipline is responsible for the recruitment and career development of specialist staff and for making decisions about their promotion and pay. While on a project, individuals are thus placed in the matrix intersection, being responsible on a day-to-day basis to the project leader but continuing to be functionally responsible to the head of their discipline.

A matrix organisation is illustrated in Figure 6.

Advantages and disadvantages of matrix organisations

The advantages of matrix organisations are that they

- enable organisations in the business of conducting

Figure 6 A matrix organisation

		Key project disciplines					
		A	B	C	D	E	F
Project team	1	√	√	√	√		√
	2	√					
	3		√	√		√	
	4	√	√	√	√	√	√
	5					√	√

projects quickly to assemble teams consisting of people with the most appropriate expertise and experience

- help to achieve excellent speed of response and flexibility in the case of new demands

- recognise that project management is a special skill and that a pool of experienced leaders needs to be maintained

- recognise the need to develop and nurture expertise in the key disciplines which the business uses in its projects

- provide a variety of experience to team members, broadening their skills base in conjunction with members of other disciplines and developing project management skills.

The disadvantages of matrix organisations are that they

- tend to be fragmented – it is difficult to develop and maintain commitment to the organisation

- can unsettle individuals, who will be constantly working for new bosses on different projects – there may be little continuity

- require individuals to be responsible to two bosses simultaneously – their project leader and the head of their discipline – which may create ambivalence

- necessitate careful planning to ensure that resources from the different disciplines are available when required without people's spending too much time idle and waiting for work

• may limit or appear to limit career progression for individuals because of those individuals' constant movement between projects and because of the consequent difficulty of developing coherent career plans.

Process-based organisation

A process-based organisation is one in which the focus is on horizontal processes that cut across organisational boundaries. Traditional organisation structures consisted of a range of functions operating semi-independently and each with its own, usually extended, management hierarchy. Functions acted as vertical 'chimneys', with boundaries between what they did and what happened next door. Continuity of work between functions and the co-ordination of activities was prejudiced. Attention was focused on vertical relationships and authority-based management – the 'command and control' structure. Horizontal processes that cut across organisational boundaries received relatively little attention. It was, for example, not recognised that meeting the needs of customers by systems of order processing could only be carried out satisfactorily if the flow of work from sales through manufacturing to distribution was treated as a continuous process and not as three distinct parcels of activity. Another horizontal process which drew attention to the need to reconsider how organisations should be structured was total quality initiatives. These are not top-down systems. They cut across the boundaries separating organisational units to ensure that quality is built into the organisation's products and services. Business process re-engineering exercises have also demonstrated the need for businesses to integrate functionally-separated tasks into unified horizontal work processes.

The result, as indicated by Ghoshal and Bartlett,[16] has been that managers are beginning to deal with their organisations in different ways. Rather than seeing them as a hierarchy of static roles, they think of them as a portfolio of dynamic processes. They see core organisational processes that overlay and often dominate the vertical, authority-based processes of the hierarchical structure.

In a process-based organisation there will still be designated functions for, say, manufacturing, sales and distribution. But the emphasis will be on how these areas work together on multi-functional projects to deal with new demands such as product/market development, or, as in Bass Taverns, commissioning new pubs. Teams will jointly consider ways of responding to customer requirements. Quality and continuous improvement will be regarded as a common responsibility shared between managers and staff from each function. The overriding objective will be to maintain a smooth flow of work between functions and to achieve synergy by pooling resources from different functions on taskforces or project teams. Part of a process-based organisation is illustrated in Figure 7.

Advantages and disadvantages of process-based organisations

The advantages of process-based organisations are that they

- provide for the smooth flow of work between and across functions to meet customer demands and enhance the thrust for quality and cost-effectiveness

Figure 7 A process–based organisation

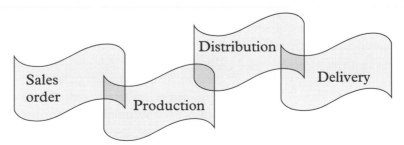

- reduce the insularity which can plague functional 'chimneys' in a traditional organisation

- enable resources to be pooled on multi-functional project teams more easily to develop new products, markets or processes.

The disadvantages of process-based organisations are that they can

- diffuse attention away from the core activities of particular functions

- lead to excessive attention to work flows rather than to what is actually produced, sold and delivered

- confuse people within and outside the organisation as to who is responsible for what

- diffuse responsibility.

THE FLEXIBLE FIRM

The concept of the flexible firm is often used generally to indicate an organisation which is able to respond quickly and flexibly to new demands generated by the market generally or by individual customers. *Job-based flexibility* means that people can be moved between different tasks and may be expected to use a wider range of skills. Rather than work at jobs, they carry out roles – behaving in appropriate ways depending on the situation. *Organisation-based flexibility* exists in core-periphery, 'shamrock' and '*ad-hoc*-racy' organisations.

Core-periphery

A core-periphery organisation is one that retains a core of permanently employed key workers who carry out the fundamental tasks which the organisation exists to do. The 'periphery' consists of part-time, casual and contract workers who are employed when they are needed, or who carry out tasks that are not basic to the organisation. This is a form of team organisation, and a move towards a core-periphery structure often means downsizing, although those retained are offered a measure of security.

'Shamrock' organisation

The 'shamrock' organisation is Handy's[17] term for a core-periphery structure. As he puts it:

> The core will be composed of well-qualified people, professionals, technicians or managers. They get most of their identity and purpose from their work. They *are* the organisation and are likely to be both committed to it and dependent on it.

In contrast, what Handy calls the 'contractual fringe' will be made up of both individuals and organisations. The individuals will be self-employed professionals or technicians, many of them past employees of the central organisation who ran out of roles in the core or who preferred the freedom of self-employment.

The core and the contractual fringe compose two leaves of the shamrock; the third leaf consists of the flexible labour force who carry out part-time or temporary work.

The '*ad-hoc*-racy'

The '*ad-hoc*-racy' is a term coined by Mintzberg[18] for organisations where, as he expresses it, 'power is decentralised selectively to constellations of workers that are free to co-ordinate within and between themselves by mutual adjustments.' As the term implies, such organisations evolve and respond as required to the circumstances in which they exist. There is no fixed or permanent structure – it is constantly being adjusted to meet new conditions. Software houses, especially in their earlier stages, often take the form of *ad-hoc*-racies.

WHERE THESE STRUCTURES CAN BE FOUND

The structures described above can be found in any organisation. The choice of structure depends on the circumstances of the business, its purpose, the views of top management and its functions in accordance with the principle that 'form follows function'. One organisation could operate entirely on a decentralised basis with the maximum amount of autonomy devolved to strategic business units. Another could centralise some activities and decentralise others. A process-based approach may operate in one part of an organisation while elsewhere a more traditional 'line-and-staff' structure may be adopted. There is no one right way of organising. Organisation design is contingent on the situation.

Charles Handy[19] writes: 'It is the organisation's job to deliver; it is not its job to be everyone's alternative community, providing for all for life.' To what extent do you agree or disagree with this statement, and why?

What type of structures might you find in the following organisations?

- a conglomerate owning a number of different but unrelated businesses
- a high-tech company in the defence industry with a strong research and development function and a computer-manufacturing system operated by technicians
- a company responsible for marketing a foreign car through a chain of distributors
- a national housing association delivering 'care' to people with learning difficulties in sheltered accommodation
- a brewing company managing a number of tied outlets
- an insurance company with a strong customer-focus
- a local authority
- a large comprehensive school
- a manufacturing company which produces a range of interrelated products that are marketed on the basis of quality and in which the key requirements are speed of response to customer requirements and effective after-sales service.

Consider your own organisation or one familiar to you. How would you describe it in terms of its type of structure?

ORGANISATION DESIGN

The process of organising may involve the grand design or re-design of the total structure, but most often it is concerned with the organisation of particular functions and activities and the basis upon which the relationships between them are managed. Organisations are not static things. Changes are constantly taking place in the business itself, in the environment in which the business operates, and in the people who work in the business. There is no such thing as an ideal organisation. The most that can be done is to optimise the processes in order to achieve the best 'fit' between the structure and the functions carried out in an ever-changing environment. This is one good reason why a flexible or decentralised approach is often desirable. It also needs to be borne in mind that although it may be possible to visualise an ideal structure, the organisation functions may have to be adjusted to fit the particular strengths and attributes of the people available – for changing and turbulent environments a flexible approach is desirable.

Approach to organisation design

Organisation design or re-design should be conducted in specific stages:

1 An *analysis* of the existing arrangements – their strengths and weaknesses in relation to the opportunities and threats facing the organisation.

2 A *diagnosis* of what needs to be done to improve the way in which the organisation functions.

3 A *plan* to implement any revisions to the structure emerging from the diagnosis, possibly in phases.

4 *Implementation* of the plan, bearing in mind that this may involve a major change management exercise as described in Chapter 16.

5 *Evaluation* of the impact of the reorganisation, and making adjustments as necessary.

Points to be covered

The things to do when designing or re-designing an organisation are:

• Identify the internal and external environmental factors which may influence the design.

• Clarify the overall purpose of the organisation.

• Define the key activities required to achieve that purpose.

• Group these activities logically together as units, teams, processes, taking into account interdependencies and the flow of work across the boundaries between possible groups.

• Define the role and function of each team, unit or process, paying particular attention to its relationship with other units so that the maximum amount of integration can be achieved.

• Decide on a management/team leader structure required to direct, co-ordinate and control activities in units or processes, and define who will be accountable for delivering results in each area.

• Define reporting relationships between managers/team leaders and the members of their teams.

• Design jobs and define roles to make the best use of the skills and capacities of those who will carry them out.

• Clarify with teams and individuals the results they are expected to achieve in terms of targets and standards of performance.

• Plan and implement organisational development activities to ensure that the various processes in the organisation operate in ways which contribute to organisational effectiveness.

Organisation guidelines

The original management theorists produced sets of principles of organisation they claimed were universally applicable. The best-known of these are 'unity of command' (no one should have more than one boss) and 'span of control' (no manager should control more than five or six subordinates whose jobs were different). Neither of these principles is wrong (having two bosses *can* create confusion, and too many people with different roles reporting to a manager *can* cause problems) but they are certainly not universally applicable. People can successfully report to both a line manager for their day-to-day activities and a functional manager for maintaining required standards and implementing company policies in their area. In today's de-layered organisations managers have to be responsible for much wider spans of control, which they achieve by delegation and empowerment and which is made easier by the ready availability of control information through computers.

There are, however, certain guidelines which are worth remembering, even if they should not be applied rigidly:

- *differentiation and integration* – Although it is necessary to differentiate between the different activities carried out, it is equally necessary to ensure that these activities are integrated and that the horizontal processes that cut across organisational processes are recognised and catered for.

- *teamwork* – Jobs and roles should be described in ways which facilitate teamwork. Areas where co-operation between functions and individuals are important should be emphasised. Networking should be encouraged.

- *decentralisation* – Authority to make decisions should be delegated as close to the scene of action as possible.

- *de-layering* – Superficial layers of management or supervision should be removed to promote flexibility and responsiveness, give people more responsibility, facilitate better communication, and cut costs.

- *role clarification* – People should be clear about their roles as individuals and members of teams.

> What are the things you would look for if you were asked to comment on the effectiveness of an organisation structure? Mintzberg[20] has commented that 'De-layering is the process of people who don't know how the organisation works getting rid of those who do.' What does he mean? Is there any validity in this opinion?

JOB DESIGN

Job design, or role definition, is the process of defining what activities are carried out by a job- or role-holder. Each activity consists of three elements: planning (deciding what to do, if there is any choice), executing (implementing the plan) and controlling (monitoring performance and progress and taking corrective action as necessary). A fully integrated role contains all these elements for each of the tasks involved.

Job design should define a job in such a way as to maximise the intrinsic motivation it provides (intrinsic motivation is the inspiration and encouragement provided by the work itself). These motivating characteristics are important:

- autonomy, discretion, self-control and responsibility
- variety
- the use of personal abilities
- feedback
- belief that the work is significant.

Overall, job design should consider the extent to which individuals can be 'empowered' by being given greater scope and responsibility for their work.

> You are the leader of a team in an insurance company servicing a number of accounts, setting them up, dealing with claims and answering enquiries. You have recommended, and it has been agreed, that a new position should be established in your line – to work full-time on providing improved services to customers. How would you approach designing this job?

HOW TO DRAW UP AN ORGANISATION CHART

Organisation charts provide a generalised illustration of the allocation of work between functions and of formal reporting relationships. But they cannot convey the reality of how a business works. All they can do is indicate in very broad terms how activities are grouped together, who is responsible for what, and who reports to whom. They may indicate direct lines of control but they cannot illustrate the cross-functional lines of communication or the fact that although individuals may be supposed ostensibly to report to a manager, they may in practice spend much of their time working for or with other people in, for example, cross-functional project teams.

Notwithstanding these caveats, organisation charts are useful ways of summing up a structure and clarifying basic responsibilities and reporting relationships. To construct one you have to

- Define who is responsible for groups of activities or a single set of related activities. These positions are placed in the boxes on the chart.

- Establish reporting relationships – the teams or individual positions which managers at the various levels direct, co-ordinate and control. These lines connect the various position boxes on the chart.

- Define any functional relationships between, for example, a plant personnel manager and the group personnel director. These are sometimes shown by a dotted line.

- Cross-reference positions to outline job descriptions or role definitions which set out in more detail what job-holders do.

> What are the limitations of a conventional organisation chart?
> What purposes can it serve?
> Draw up an organisation chart for your company or function, without reference to any existing chart.

HOW TO WRITE A JOB DESCRIPTION

Job descriptions (also known as 'accountability profiles' or 'role definitions') provide more detailed information on how organisations function. They also serve other important purposes: defining accountabilities for performance management, indicating the areas in which targets should be set, and providing the basis for competence analysis and employee development and job evaluation.

The aim should be to keep the job description short and simple – ideally on the classic one side of one sheet of paper. The days of elaborate descriptions that prescribe and describe every duty in great detail are gone.

The description should consist of three parts:

1 *Job purpose* – a one sentence definition of the overall purpose of the job – what it exists to do

2 *Reporting relationships* – who the job-holder reports to and who reports to the job-holder

3 *Key result areas* (also called 'principal accountabilities', 'main activities' or 'key tasks') – a description of the essence of the job in terms of the main areas in which the job-holder has to achieve results. There are normally no more than seven or eight key result areas in any job, however senior or complex it is. Each key result area or accountability should be described in one clause beginning with an active verb – 'plans', 'prepares', 'provides', 'despatches', etc. The object of the verb (what is done) is set out as briefly as possible: 'despatches planned output to the warehouse' (*how* it is done does not have to be described). Finally, the purpose of the activity is stated in terms of outputs or standards: 'despatches the warehouse planned output so that all items are removed by carrier within 24 hours of their being packed'.

An example of a job description

Personnel Manager

Job purpose

to provide advice and cost-effective personnel services which enable the company to achieve its goals and meet its responsibilities to the people it employs

Reporting relationships

- reports to: plant manager

- reporting to role-holder: personnel officer, training officer, personal assistant

Key result areas

1 Advise on personnel strategies, policies and practices which support the achievement of the company's business objectives while fulfilling its obligations to employees.

2 Provide a recruitment and selection service to meet the company's needs.

3 Provide advice on all employment and health and safety matters, including issues arising in connection with employment legislation, to ensure that the company meets its legal and social obligations and avoids legal actions.

4 Develop and help to maintain performance-management processes which are owned by line managers and employees, and make a significant contribution to employee motivation, performance and development.

5 Plan and implement employee development programmes to meet identified needs, and satisfy the company's requirements for an effective and multiskilled workforce.

6 Advise on reward management systems and the

operation of the company's pay structure and performance pay schemes which obtain, retain and motivate employees.

7 Advise on employee relations issues and co-ordinate the company's involvement and communication processes in order to develop and maintain a co-operative and peaceful climate of employee relations in the company.

8 Develop and maintain an effective computerised personnel information system.

Job descriptions may be extended to become role definitions by listing the key competencies job holders have to possess in terms of their role.

Consider your own job or any other and draw up a job description along the lines described above.

ORGANISATIONAL DEVELOPMENT

Organisational development is concerned with the planning and implementation of programmes designed to improve the effectiveness with which an organisation functions and responds to change. The aim is to adopt a coherent approach which enhances the ways in which people carry out their work, especially in the ways in which they interact with others. The starting-point of an organisational development programme is an understanding of what constitutes organisational effectiveness. The next stages are analysis and diagnosis, followed by the design and implementation of organisational development programmes.

Organisational effectiveness

An effective organisation is one that achieves its purpose

by meeting the needs and expectations of its stakeholders. The characteristics of an effective organisation include the following, as defined by Beckhard:[21]

1 The organisation and its teams and individual contributors manage their work against goals and plans for the achievement of these goals.

2 Form follows function – the activity, task or project determines how people are organised.

3 Decisions are made by and near the source of information.

4 Communication laterally and vertically is relatively undistorted. People are generally open and share relevant facts.

5 There is a minimum amount of inappropriate win/lose activity between individuals and groups.

6 There may be some clash of ideas about tasks and projects but relatively little over interpersonal difficulties because they have been worked through.

Analysis and diagnosis

The analysis of organisations from a developmental point of view can follow broadly the headings set out by Beckhard as listed above, with one additional point. The main questions to ask are:

1 To what extent is the organisation goal-oriented, with clearly-defined objectives which strongly influence plans and activities at all levels?

2 Does the organisation structure properly reflect the nature of the work and the activities carried out? Are there any ambiguities? Has sufficient account been taken of the need for flexibility and the flow of processes across organisational boundaries?

3 To what extent is decision-making devolved in the organisation close to the scene of action? How much authority have units and individuals got? Is it sufficient,

too much, or too little? To what extent have teams and individuals been empowered to take responsibility?

4 How effectively do communication flows work in the organisation – laterally as well as diagonally? To what extent are people open with one another and to what extent do they share relevant information?

5 How much unnecessary conflict is there in the organisation? Do people indulge in inappropriate win/lose activities? To what extent do politics and power-ploys influence the way the organisation operates?

6 How much interpersonal conflict is there? To what extent is there evidence that people work through differences of opinion?

7 How effectively do team members work with one another? How well do teams co-operate with one another?

This analysis can be conducted by the processes of 'action research', which takes the form of collecting data from people about process issues such as those listed above. This can be carried on into a diagnostic phase by feeding reactions back to people to identify the likely causes of problems so that possible actions can be tested.

The diagnosis arising from the analysis can lead to various types of organisation-development activities or pro-grammes (sometimes called 'OD interventions') as summarised below.

Organisational development activities
Typical organisational development activities include:

- introducing new structures or processes

- working with teams on team development

- working on inter-group relationships, either in defining roles or resolving inter-group conflict

- change-management programmes

- various learning activities to help people improve their personal or inter-personal skills.

Jack Welch, chief executive officer of the General Electrical Company, has stated that he wants to achieve a 'boundaryless organisation'. What does he mean by this phrase, and why might it be important in a massive and successful manufacturing company?

A direct marketing organisation has two departments carrying out research into consumer preferences and choices. Internally, the operations research department analyses information about buying habits and trends from the database. Externally, the market research department conducts special projects to identify who customers are, what they prefer to buy, and what type of service they want. There is conflict between the needs of the two departments. Each of them claims that the other is encroaching on its territory and each believes that it should be entirely responsible for all internal and external research. They are both highly competent in their field and are delivering excellent information. How would you deal with this situation?

SUMMARY

- Organisation structures define and clarify how required activities are grouped together, who is responsible to whom for what, and the lines of authority.

- Organisations function according to the situations in which they exist, with an increasing emphasis on flexibility and process.

- Organisations necessarily contain specialists, but they have to fit into teams.

- Autonomy is a desirable feature in organisations, but there are limits to the extent to which it can be granted to units, teams or individuals.

- The formal organisation is the structure defined in an organisation chart, but this creates and requires informal organisation – the network of relationships that make organisations work.

- Organisations may be:
  - unitary, with basic and very clearly-defined boundaries

- divisionalised, with discrete units or functions responsible for a range of associated activities
- centralised or decentralised, with authority concentrated at the centre or devolved to a greater or lesser degree to strategic business units (SBUs)
- matrix, with projects staffed by people drawn from different disciplines who are responsible to the project leader for their work on the project and also to the head of their discipline for employment, deployment and career development
- process-based, with the focus on horizontal processes which cut across organisational boundaries
- flexible, operating with a permanent core of key employees and a periphery of contract and temporary workers, or functioning as an 'ad-hoc-racy' responding to particular demands as required.

• Organisation design will produce structures that are contingent on the circumstances and the environment of the organisation. The design process is concerned with identifying and grouping activities, defining who is responsible for what to whom, and establishing reporting relationships and lines of control.

• Job design is the process of deciding what activities should be carried out by a job-holder. It pays attention to the planning, executing and controlling aspects of the work, and how the job can be defined in a way which maximises intrinsic motivation.

• Organisation development is concerned with the analysis and diagnosis of the factors that determine organisational effectiveness, and the planning and delivery of programmes to increase that effectiveness.

REFERENCES

1 TRIST E. L., HIGGIN G. W., MURRAY H. *and* POLLACK A. B. *Organisational Choice.* London, Tavistock, 1963.
2 FAYOL H. *Administration Industrielle et Générale.* Translated by C. STORRS as *General and Industrial Management.* London, Pitman, 1949.

3 TAYLOR F. W. *Principles of Scientific Management.* New York, Harper, 1911.

4 URWICK F. L. *Dynamic Administration.* London, Pitman, 1947.

5 WEBER M. *From Max Weber.* H. H. GERTH *and* C. W. MILLS (eds), Oxford, Oxford University Press, 1946.

6 BURNS T. *and* STALKER G. *The Management of Innovation.* London, Tavistock, 1961.

7 WOODWARD J. *Industrial Organisation.* Oxford, Oxford University Press, 1965.

8 LAWRENCE P. R. *and* LORSCH J. W. *Developing Organisations.* Reading, Mass., Addison Wesley, 1969.

9 PASCALE R. *Managing on the Edge.* London, Viking, 1990.

10 HANDY C. *The Age of Unreason.* London, Business Books, 1989.

11 BARNARD C. *The Functions of an Executive.* Boston, Mass., Harvard University Press, 1938.

12 CHILD J. *Organisation: A guide to problems and practice.* London, Harper & Row, 1977.

13 BURNS *and* STALKER, see Note 6 above.

14 GOOLD M. *and* CAMPBELL A. *Strategies and Styles: The role of the centre in managing diversified corporations.* Oxford, Blackwell, 1986.

15 SLOAN A. O. *My Years With General Motors.* New York, Doubleday, 1963.

16 GHOSHAL S. *and* BARTLETT C. A. 'Changing the role of top management: beyond structure to process', *Harvard Business Review,* January–February 1995; pp. 86–96.

17 HANDY, see Note 10 above.

18 MINTZBERG H. 'Organisation design: fashion or fit', *Harvard Business Review,* January–February 1981; pp. 103–116.

19 HANDY, see Note 10 above.

20 MINTZBERG, see Note 18 above.

21 BECKHARD R. *Organisation Development: Strategy and models.* Reading, Mass., Addison-Wesley, 1969.

10 Authority, power, politics and conflict in organisations

Formal organisation structures as described in the last chapter may define the framework for getting things done, but the ways in which people behave in their roles – the processes of exercising power and authority, acting politically, and, inevitably, conflicting with others – affect *how* things get done.

On completing this chapter, a reader will understand how these various processes operate and how they affect organisational behaviour.

AUTHORITY

Authority is defined by the *Oxford English Dictionary* as the 'power or right to enforce obedience'. This rather fierce definition could be modified to read: '*authority* is the process of exerting influence on others in order to get things done.' This is sometimes referred to as the 'authority to command'. Such influence can be achieved by the exercise of power or by more subtle means. According to the classic school of management theorists, such as Fayol,[1] organisations achieve order and regularity by the use of authority implemented through a defined hierarchy or chain of command. This 'command and control' approach to the use of authority is regarded with distaste by most recent writers on organisation. Handy[2] advocates the development of a 'culture of consent' in which the emphasis is on the virtues of decentralisation, empowerment and self-managed teams.

But organisations do contain 'regularly occurring features which help to shape their members' behaviour' (Child[3]), and one of these features is the use of authority. Ultimately, organisations exist to get things done, and this will involve exercising authority, although this may take place in the form of management by agreement rather than management by control.

Authority can be structured – vested in the role of manager – or it may be based on expertise or personal charisma. There is also moral authority exercised on the basis of the 'rightness' of the action because it is ethical, fair or equitable. It is possible to distinguish, as Cooper[4] does, between authority exercised by people with expertise who are respected as such and authority based simply on position. Cooper coined the phrase 'authentic authority' which corresponds to a form of control that is not exercised by dominating others. It differs from *power* in the sense that people will respond willingly to authentic authority based on expertise (a culture of consent), whereas power requires compliance even if they disagree.

Leaders exercise authority, but only in Handy's[5] sense: 'A leader shapes and shares a vision which gives point to the work of others ... The vision remains a dream without the work of others. A leader with no followers is a voice in the wilderness.' Handy describes what he calls 'a post-heroic leader' as one who 'asks how every problem can be solved in a way that develops other people's capacity to handle it'.

The term 'authority' also refers to the right to make decisions or take action (authority to act), and this right may be authorised by a more senior manager (authority to authorise).

> What are people doing when they exercise authority?
> What is meant by the phrase: 'He/she has exceeded his/her authority'?
> How can the authority to act be defined?

POWER

Nietzsche said that 'power has crooked legs'; Wilhelm Reich wrote that it is repression – 'a relation of force'; and Jay[6] commented that

> Power lies in the acceptance of your authority by others – their knowledge that if they try to resist you, they will fail and you will succeed.

Power is the capacity to impress the dominance of one's goals or values on others. Four different types of power have been identified by French and Raven:[7]

- *reward power* – derived from the belief of individuals that compliance brings rewards; the ability to distribute rewards contributes considerably to an executive's power

- *coercive power* – stemming from a conviction that non-compliance will bring punishment

- *expert power* – exercised by people who are popular or admired and with whom the less powerful can identify

- *legitimised power* – power conferred by position in an organisation.

Cyert and March[8] developed a behavioural view of the firm as a coalition of individuals who are, in turn, members of sub-coalitions, each with different goals. There will, however, be a dominant coalition which will use power to impose its goals in the organisation.

Foucault,[9] who wrote and spoke extensively about the concept of power, described it as ubiquitous and comprehensive: 'Power is a machine in which everyone is caught, those who exercise it just as much as those over whom it is exercised.' He regarded the disciplinary drive as being particularly widely spread in bourgeois society (one of its great inventions), as exemplified by the control of the daily activities of workers. But Foucault did not always think of power as negative (although his views on this subject varied):

> We must cease once and for all to describe the effects of power in negative terms: it 'excludes', it 'represses', it 'censors', it 'abstracts', it 'masks', it 'conceals'. In fact, power produces; it produces reality; it produces domains of object and rituals of truth. The individual and the knowledge that may be gained of him [*sic*] belong to this production.

He also pointed out the intimate connection between knowledge and power: 'To know something is to create a new power relationship.'

Exercising power responsibly

The responsible use of power occurs when managers do their best not to coerce people into taking action against their will. If something has to be done because it has been ordered by higher authority or because there is a crisis, such managers at least explain why the action is necessary, and request and listen to suggestions about the method of proceeding. When these conditions do not exist, power is exercised responsibly wherever a 'culture of consent' is nurtured. This is when a manager gets people involved in discussing courses of action and work methods. It also means that the manager takes steps to 'empower' people. Empowering is the process of giving people more scope (or 'power') to exercise control over, and take responsibility for, their work. The manager thus devolves authority, delegating more, and allowing individuals and teams more scope to plan, to act independently, and to monitor their own performance.

Is the exercise of power ever legitimate? If so, in what circumstances?

Is it fair to say that power equals coercion? If so, why?

Foucault tells us that power is pervasive. What does he mean by that statement?

Why is the concept of power a factor to be considered when trying to understand the behavioural forces operating in organisations?

POLITICS

Power and politics are inextricably mixed, and in any organisation there will inevitably be people who want to achieve satisfaction by acquiring power, legitimately or illegitimately. They may do this by 'playing politics'. Political behaviour in organisations involves finding out who has the decision-making power and how decisions are made so that influence – which is often hidden – can be exerted without going through normal channels. Political behaviour in organisations has been described by Kakabadse[10] as 'a process, that of influencing individuals and groups of people to your own point of view, where you cannot rely on authority'. To be 'politic', according to the *Oxford English Dictionary*, you should be sagacious, prudent, judicious, expedient, scheming or crafty. So by this definition political behaviour in an organisation might be either desirable or undesirable. But it is the 'expedient', 'scheming' and 'crafty' aspects of political behaviour that makes it suspect even when it is widespread.

A political approach on the part of a manager means that he or she is aware of where power is based in the organisation, who are members of the dominant coalition, who holds the power, and who makes the key decisions. Organisational politicians know that such decisions are often made behind closed doors or by a coterie of people who are in the know and are in positions of power and influence. They know whom they should influence – and the best way to do so.

The essence of political behaviour is that it is not open behaviour. It is discreet. Organisational politicians exert hidden influence to get their way. They are 'politically sensitive' – they are aware of what is going on behind the scenes, who is a rising star, whose reputation is fading, and the less obvious factors that are likely to affect decisions. They use that knowledge to make things happen *their* way by exerting influence in the right quarter. Organisational politicians do not 'go through channels': they intrigue, they form factions, they go behind people's backs, they lobby (although sounding out opinion is often desirable before plunging into a proposal).

Put like this, political behaviour sounds unethical. But some organisations are webs of political intrigue – and in others, progress cannot be made *unless* the political climate within the organisation is understood and people act in the light of that understanding. It may be quite justifiable to sound out opinion and to line up support (to do a bit of lobbying) if you are about to launch what may be a contentious proposal at a meeting. Political systems exist and managers may find themselves having to operate within those systems.

But political behaviour can be subversive, divisive and counterproductive. It can create a climate of intrigue in which decisions are no longer visible and where people with more political nous do better than the straightforward organisational citizens who are simply and openly doing a good job. However, in the real world in which managers live, it is at least necessary to appreciate that decision-making in organisations is not always as transparent as it might be. Political sensitivity in this case means knowing 'how things are done around here', knowing how decisions are made, knowing who makes the running – and bearing all this in mind when faced with situations in which proposals have to be made or actions taken.

Organisations consist of individuals who, while they are ostensibly there to achieve a common purpose, are at the same time driven by their own needs to achieve their own goals. Effective management is the process of harmonising individual endeavour and ambition to the common good. Some individuals genuinely believe that using political means to achieve their goals will benefit the organisation as well as themselves. Yet others unashamedly pursue their own ends.

It can be argued that a political approach to management is inevitable and even desirable in an organisation in which the clarity of goals is not absolute, where the decision-making process is not clear cut and where the authority to make decisions is not evenly or appropriately distributed. There can be few organisations in which one or more of these conditions do not apply. In this sense, it could be argued that a political approach can be legitimate as long as the ends are justifiable from the viewpoint of the organisation. But organisational politicians can subvert the proper ways in which decisions should be made, where the emphasis is on transparency and public accountability.

Can you think of any circumstances when political behaviour would be appropriate in an organisation?
What can go wrong if politics are rife in an organisation?
What is meant by 'political sensitivity'? Is it a quality that is worth developing? If so, how?

CONFLICT

Conflict takes place in organisations because organisations function by means of adjustments and compromises among competitive elements in their structure and membership. People's views often conflict. If they hold them strongly, the result can be two kinds of conflict: horizontal between functions, departments, groups and individuals, and vertical between different levels in the hierarchy.

Conflict also arises when there is change, because change may be seen as a threat to be challenged or resisted. Or conflict can arise when there is frustration – this may produce an aggressive reaction: fight rather than flight. Conflict should not always be deplored. It is an inevitable result of progress and change. It would be strange if everyone's views in an organisation coincided. Conflict can and should be used constructively to bring issues out into the open and, through discussion, to arrive at a better solution or course of action.

Conflict between individuals raises fewer problems than conflict between groups. Individuals can act independently and resolve their differences. Members of groups may have to accept the norms, goals, and values of their group. An individual's loyalty will usually be to his or her own group if it is in conflict with others.

Resolving conflict

As Mary Parker Follett[11] wrote, there is the possibility that conflict can be creative if an integrative approach is used to settle it. This means clarifying priorities, policies and roles, using agreed procedures to deal with grievances and disputes, bringing differences of interpretation out into the open, and achieving consensus through a solution which recognises the interests of both parties – a win/win process. Resolving conflict by the sheer exercise of power (win/lose) will only lead to further conflict. Resolving conflict by compromise may lead to both parties being dissatisfied (lose/lose).

The best method of handling conflict is to adopt a problem-solving approach by

- getting agreement on what the problem is

- jointly analysing the causes of the conflict

- identifying alternative means of dealing with the issue

- jointly evaluating the merits of each alternative from the perspectives of both parties

- working through the alternatives to find the one closest to meeting the needs of everyone concerned

- agreeing on how the preferred solution can be implemented to the satisfaction of both parties.

Do you believe that conflict is inevitable in organisations? If so, why?

In manufacturing organisations conflict can exist between the sales and production departments. Sales can accuse production of not fulfilling orders quickly enough and therefore of letting them down with their customers. Production can accuse sales of over-selling (not being aware of lead times) or of making impossible demands. What might be done to resolve this conflict?

SUMMARY

- Authority is the process of exerting influence on others in order to get things done.

- Authority can be exercised by means of a 'command and control' approach. But writers such as Charles Handy advocate the development of a 'culture of consent' in which the emphasis is on the virtues of decentralisation, empowerment and self-managed teams.

- Authority can be structured – vested in the role of manager – or it may be based on expertise or personal charisma. There is also moral authority exercised on the basis of the 'rightness' of the action because it is ethical, fair or equitable.

- In Cooper's phrase, 'authentic authority' is not exercised through dominating others. It differs from 'power' in the sense that people will respond willingly to authentic authority based on expertise (a culture of consent), whereas power demands compliance even if disagreed with.

- Power is the capacity to impress the dominance of one's goals or values on others. The four different types of power have been identified by French and Raven as reward power, coercive power, expert power, and legitimised power.

- Politics is described by Kakabadse as 'a process, that of influencing individuals and groups of people to your own point of view, where you cannot rely on authority'.

- A political approach means that managers (and others) are aware of where power is based in the organisation: who are members of the dominant coalition, who holds the power, who makes the key decisions.

- The essence of political behaviour is that it is not open behaviour. It is discreet. Organisational politicians exert hidden influence to get their way.

- Conflict is inevitable. It takes place in organisations because they function by means of adjustments and compromises among competitive elements in their structure and membership.

- The best method of handling conflict is to adopt a problem-solving approach which involves getting agreement on what the problem is, jointly analysing the causes of the conflict, identifying and evaluating alternative means of dealing with the issue to find the one which is closest to meeting the needs of everyone concerned, and agreeing on how the preferred solution can be implemented to the satisfaction of both parties.

REFERENCES

1 FAYOL H. *General and Industrial Administration*. London, Pitman, 1949.
2 HANDY C. *The Age of Unreason*. London, Business Books, 1989.

3 CHILD J. *Organisation: A guide to problems and practice*. London, Harper & Row, 1977.

4 COOPER D. 'The anti-hospital: an experiment in psychiatry'. *New Society*, March 1965; pp. 4–6.

5 HANDY, see Note 2 above.

6 JAY A. *Management and Machiavelli*. London, Hodder & Stoughton, 1967.

7 FRENCH J. R. *and* RAVEN B. 'The basis of social power', in CARTWRIGHT D. (ed.) *Studies in Social Power*. Ann Arbor, Mich., Institute for Social Research, 1959.

8 CYERT R. M. *and* MARCH J. G. *A Behavioural View of the Firm*. Englewood Cliffs, New Jersey, Prentice-Hall, 1963.

9 FOUCAULT M. *Power/Knowledge: Selected interviews and other writings*. Brighton, The Harvester Press, 1981.

10 KAKABADSE A. *The Politics of Management*. Aldershot, Gower, 1983.

11 FOLLETT M. P. *Creative Experience*. London, Pitman, 1924.

11 Organisational communications

Organisational communications correspond to the various methods organisations use to inform employees about matters management believes to be important. Good organisational communications can be a valuable means of increasing commitment. On completing this chapter, a reader will recognise and be familiar with:

- the need for communications

- the nature of organisational communications

- barriers to communicaitons

- the various channels available.

THE NEED FOR ORGANISATIONAL COMMUNICATIONS

Organisations want to obtain the commitment of their employees. Managements would like people to identify with the goals and values of the organisation, to want to belong to it, and to work hard on its behalf. To develop a well-committed workforce it is necessary to create and maintain an effective system of two-way communications: from management to employees and back from employees to management. Management needs to explain its values and expectations. Employees need to have the chance to raise issues and questions directly with their managers without necessarily having to go through formal consultative channels.

The organisation in particular has to recognise that it functions by means of the collective action of people, yet each individual is capable of taking independent action which may not be in line with policy or organisational needs, or may not be reported properly to other people who ought to know about it. Good communications are required to achieve co-ordinated results.

Communications consist of the transmission of instructions, comments and suggestions, and the exchange of information in writing, by word of mouth or through a computer system.

THE NATURE OF ORGANISATIONAL COMMUNICATIONS

Organisational communications are concerned with the creation, transmission, interpretation and use of information. The communication can be on a person-to-person basis, as when information is exchanged between people, a manager asks someone to do something, colleagues exchange information, or someone informs his or her manager that something has been done. Or it can be on a departmental/corporate basis, as when general instructions or pieces of information are passed down the line, and reactions, reports and comments float, more or less effectively, up again.

Communications can be oral, in writing or conducted through e-mail, videos, computer-conferencing and computer reports on hard copy or distributed to a network of micro-computers or VDUs.

Communications start with a communicator's wanting to convey something to another person, to a group of people or to a whole organisation or organisational unit. The communicator then decides how it is to be expressed and transmitted. The resultant communication reaches the recipients, who form an impression of what they have read or heard and interpret it against their own background of attitudes and experiences.

One basic problem in communications is that the meaning actually apprehended by a recipient may not be what the communicator intended to send. The communicator and the recipient are two people living in different worlds; any number of things can happen to distort messages that pass between them. People's needs and experiences tend to colour what they see and hear. Messages they do not want to hear are repressed. Others are magnified, created out of thin air or distorted. There are a number of barriers to communications.

BARRIERS TO COMMUNICATIONS

So many barriers exist to good communications that the constant cry in all organisations to the effect that communications are terrible is hardly to be wondered at – it is amazing that any undistorted messages ever get through. Some of the main barriers are summarised below.

Hearing what we expect to hear

What we hear or understand when someone speaks to us is largely based on our own experience and background. Instead of hearing what people tell us, we tend to hear what our minds tell us they have said. We all have preconceived ideas of what people mean – when we hear something new, we tend to relate it to something similar we have experienced in the past. When we receive a communication that is consistent with our own beliefs, we accept it as valid, seek additional information and remember accurately what we heard. But we tend to ignore or reject communications that conflict with our own beliefs. If they are not rejected, some way is found of twisting and shaping their meaning to fit our preconceptions. Communication often fails when it runs counter to other information that the recipient already possesses, whether that information is true or false.

Perceptions about the communicator

Recipients not only evaluate what they hear in terms of their own background, they also take the sender into account. Experience or prejudice may ascribe non-existent motives to the communicator. Some people see every collective action as a plot to get something done in an underhand way – the 'conspiracy theory' of organisational (or political) behaviour. Others look behind the message to read into it all sorts of motives different from those apparent on the surface.

The influence of one's own reference group

The group with which we identify – the reference group – influences our attitudes and feelings. 'Management' and 'the union' as well as our work group, family, ethnic set, political party and religious affiliation (if any) all constitute reference groups and colour our reactions to information. What each group hears depends on its own interests. Shared experiences and common frames of reference have more influence than messages containing information which conflicts with what employees already believe, from managers with whom they feel they have nothing in common.

Words mean different things to different people

Words may have symbolic meanings for some people, with the result that they convey a quite different impression from the one intended. Profits, to management, for example, are a prerequisite for survival and growth: to employees, they may represent ill-gotten gains from keeping down pay or overpricing. Do not assume that something which has a certain meaning to you will convey the same meaning to someone else.

The emotional context

Our emotions colour our ability to convey or to receive the true message. When we are insecure or worried, what we hear and see seems more threatening than when we are secure and at peace with the world. When we are angry or depressed, we tend to reject out of hand what might otherwise seem like reasonable requests or good ideas. During arguments, many things can be said that are not understood or are badly distorted.

Noise

'Noise', in the sense of outside factors that interfere with the reception of the message, is an obvious barrier. It may be literal noise which prevents words from being heard, or figurative noise in the shape of distracting or confused information which distorts the message. The awkward forms in which messages are communicated – unclear syntax, unwieldy sentences full of long words – all help to produce noise.

Organisational size

The sheer size and complexity of modern organisations is one of the main barriers to communication. In the traditional hierarchical organisation messages have to penetrate layer upon layer of management or move between different functions, units, or locations. They thus become distorted or never arrive. Reliance is placed more on the written than the spoken word to get the message through, and this seriously restricts the effectiveness of the communication. Reducing this problem is, of course, one of the good reasons for de-layering an organisation, although cost considerations generally come first.

> Can you think of examples of any of the above barriers to communication in an organisation you know?

OVERCOMING BARRIERS TO COMMUNICATION

The overall implication of this formidable collection of barriers is that no one should assume that every message sent will be received in the form intended. But communications can be improved as suggested below, even if perfect understanding between people is impossible.

Adjusting to the world of the receiver

When you communicate, the tendency is to adjust to yourself. You have the need to say something and to say it in a particular way. But to get the message across, you have to adjust to your recipients. This means thinking ahead and trying to work out how they will grasp the message – understanding their needs and potential reactions. It also means using feedback and reinforcement techniques, as discussed later.

Using feedback

Feedback is the process of obtaining information on what has been happening in order to take action where necessary. In communications, feedback means ensuring that communicators get a message back from the recipient which tells them how much has been understood. This is why face-to-face communication is so much more effective than the written word, as long as the communication is truly two-way – in other words, when the recipients are given adequate opportunity to respond and react.

Using reinforcement

A message may have to be presented in a number of different ways to get it across. Good speakers know that if they can get more than three important ideas across in a 30-minute talk, they are lucky, and that they must repeat each idea at least three times in different ways to ensure that the message has been received and understood. In giving complicated directions it is wise to repeat them, perhaps in different ways, to guarantee successful transmission.

Using direct, simple language

This seems so obvious as to be hardly worth stating – but many people seem unable to express themselves clearly and without the use of jargon or an excessive number of adjectives, adverbs and sub-clauses.

Reinforcing words with actions

Communications are effective only if they are credible. If management says a thing, then it must mean it and do something about it. Next time it is more likely to be believed. The motto should be 'Suit the action to the words.'

Using different channels of communication

Some communications have to be in writing to get the message across promptly and without any danger of variations in the way it is delivered. But wherever possible, written communications should be supplemented by the spoken word. Conversely, an oral briefing should be reinforced by a written confirmation.

Reducing problems of size

Communication problems arising from organisational size can be reduced structurally by cutting down the number of levels of management, reducing spans of control, creating self-managed teams, generally ensuring that activities are grouped on the basis of ease of intercommunication, and decentralising authority into smaller, self-contained (although accountable) units.

> Bearing in mind the barriers to communication and the possible ways of dealing with them listed above, what ways would you take to deal with the barriers when deciding what to do about communications in your organisation?

COMMUNICATIONS STRATEGY

To achieve good results, communication should be seen as a strategic matter to be planned, developed and controlled on the basis of a full understanding of the requirements, problems and needs of everyone in the organisation.

The starting-point for the formulation of a communications strategy should be an analysis of the different types of communication with which it should be concerned. Communication studies embrace all human activities in an organisation, and the analysis must narrow the field down to well-defined areas in which action can be taken. The strategy should be based on analyses of:

- *what management wants to say* – Management usually aims to achieve three things: first, to get employees to understand and accept what management proposes to do in areas that affect them; second, to obtain the commitment of employees to the objectives, plans and values of the organisation; and third, to help employees to appreciate more clearly the contribution they can make to organisational success and how it will benefit them.

- *what employees want to hear* – Employees want to hear about and to comment upon the matters that affect their interests. These will include changes in working methods and conditions, changes in the arrangements for overtime and shift-working, company plans which may affect pay or security, and changes in the terms and conditions of their employment.

The strategy will be concerned with the use of involvement processes, including team briefing, and formal written communication systems as discussed in the next two sections.

> What conflicts might arise between what management wants to say and what employees want to hear? How would you resolve them?

INVOLVEMENT

Employee-involvement processes such as consultative committees and team briefings provide important channels for two-way communication. Involvement can vary according to the level at which it takes place, the degree to which decision-making is shared, and the mechanisms of a greater or lesser degree of formality that are used.

Levels

Involvement can take place at the job level between team leaders and their teams. Processes at this level include the communication of information about work and the interchange of ideas about how the work should be done; these processes are essentially informal.

At management level, involvement can entail sharing information and decision-making on issues that affect the way in which work is planned and carried out, and working arrangements and conditions.

At the policy-making level, where the direction in which the business is going is determined, total involvement would imply sharing the power to make key decisions. This is not much practised in the UK.

Mechanisms for involvement

At the job level, involvement is usually informal. Teams are called together on an *ad hoc* basis to consider a particular problem or to digest and comment on new information. More formality can be injected by the use of team briefing, as described below.

At the next higher level, more formality may be appropriate in larger organisations. There is scope for the use of consultative committees or departmental councils provided with defined terms of reference on the matters they can discuss.

At the enterprise level, company or works councils can be set up.

Team briefings

The concept of a team briefing (previously called a briefing group), as originally developed by the Industrial Society, is a device to overcome the restricted nature of joint consultative committees by involving everyone in an organisation, level by level, in face-to-face meetings to present, receive and discuss information. Team briefings aim to overcome the gaps and inadequacies of casual briefings by injecting some order into the system.

Team briefings operate by setting up groups at each level in the organisation. The subjects covered are:

- *policies* – explanations of new or changed policies

- *plans* – as they affect the organisation as a whole and as they affect the immediate group

- *progress* – how the organisation and the group is getting on

- *people* – new appointments, points about personnel matters (policies, pay, security, etc).

Team briefings work to a brief prepared by the board on

key issues which is then cascaded down the organisation. The briefing meetings should, however, allow for discussion of the brief, and should also ensure that any reactions or comments are in turn fed back to the top. This provides for two-way communication.

> What are the major difficulties an organisation is likely to be faced with when attempting to improve the quality of communications through employee involvement? How might they be overcome?

FORMAL WRITTEN COMMUNICATION SYSTEMS

Formal communication systems use the written word as relayed in magazines, newsletters and bulletins and on notice-boards. The aim should be to make judicious use of a number of channels to make sure that the message gets across. These channels should be supplemented by direct spoken communications which can be structured in the form of team briefings (as described above).

Magazines

Glossy magazines or house journals are an obvious way to keep employees informed about the company and are often used for public-relations purposes as well. They can extol and explain the achievements of the company and may thus help to increase identification and even loyalty. If employees are encouraged to contribute (although this may be difficult), the magazine may take on a more human face. The biggest danger in publishing this sort of magazine is that it becomes a public-relations exercise that is seen by employees as having little relevance to their everyday affairs.

Newsletters

Newsletters aim to appear more frequently and to angle their contents more towards the immediate concerns of employees than the glossier form of house magazine. To be effective they should include articles specifically aimed at explaining what management is planning to do and how this affects everyone. They can also include more chatty human-interest material about the doings of employees to capture the attention of readers. Correspondence columns can provide an avenue for the expression of employees' views and replies from management, but no attempt should be made to censor letters (except those that are purely abusive) or to pull any punches in reply. Anonymous letters should be published if the writer gives his or her name to the editor.

Bulletins

Bulletins can be used to give employees immediate information that cannot wait for the next issue of a newsletter. Or they can be a substitute for a formal publication if the company does not feel that the greater expense is justified. Bulletins are useful only if they are distributed quickly and are seen by all interested employees. They can simply be posted on notice-boards or, more effectively, given to individual employees and used as a starting-point for a briefing session if they contain information of sufficient interest to merit a face-to-face discussion.

Videos

Specially-made videos can be a cost-effective method of getting personal messages across (eg from the chief executives) or relaying information about how the company is doing. They can, however, be regarded by employees as too slick to have any real personal impact.

Evaluate the respective merits of the above channels of communication. Which are most likely to be effective and why?

SUMMARY

• Organisational communications correspond to the various methods organisations use to inform employees of matters management believes to be important, together with the processes for obtaining the views of employees on matters that affect them. Communications are concerned with the creation, transmission and use of information.

• Barriers to communications include such personal effects as hearing only what we expect to hear, perceptions about the communicator, the influence of colleagues (the reference group), the fact that words mean different things to different people, the emotional context of the communication and 'noise' (interference), as well as the size or complexity of the organisation.

• Overcoming barriers means adapting to the world of the recipient – using feedback, using reinforcement, using direct, simple language, reinforcing words with actions, using different channels of communication, and taking structural steps to reduce problems that arise from organisational size or complexity.

• To achieve good results, communication should be seen as a strategic matter to be planned, developed and controlled on the basis of a full understanding of the requirements, problems and needs of everyone in the organisation.

• Employee involvement processes such as consultative committees and team briefings provide important channels for two-way communication. Involvement can vary according to the level at which it takes place, the degree to which decision-making is shared, and the extent to which mechanisms of a greater or lesser degree of formality are used.

• Formal communication systems using the written word are represented by magazines, newsletters, bulletins and notice-boards. The aim should be to make judicious use of a number of channels to make sure that the message gets across.

12 Managing health and safety at work

It is estimated by the Health and Safety Executive that in the UK about 500 people are killed at work every year and several hundred thousand more are injured or suffer ill-health. It is also estimated that, apart from the pain and misery caused to those directly or indirectly concerned, the total cost to British employers of work-related injury and illness exceeds £4 billion a year.

The achievement of a healthy and safe place of work and the elimination to the maximum extent possible of hazards to health and safety are the responsibility of everyone employed in an organisation, including those working there under contract. But the onus is on management to achieve and, indeed, go beyond the high standard in health and safety matters required by the legislation – the Health and Safety at Work (etc) Act 1974, and the various regulations laid down in the Codes of Practice.

The importance of healthy and safe policies and practices is, sadly, often under-estimated by those concerned with managing businesses and by individual managers within those businesses. But it cannot be emphasised too strongly that the prevention of accidents and elimination of health and safety hazards are a prime responsibility of management and managers in order to minimise suffering and loss.

At the end of this chapter a reader will understand and be able to explain:

- the importance of health and safety in the workplace
- the basic legislative requirements concerning health and safety at work
- the use of health and safety codes of practice
- the importance and content of health and safety policies

- methods of conducting risk assessments, safety audits and inspections

- methods of minimising health hazards (occupational health procedures) and preventing accidents

- how to investigate accidents

- methods of measuring health and safety performance

- how to promote healthy and safe working practices through communications and training, and the approach that can be used to advise a group of staff on the importance of health and safety in the workplace

- who is responsible for health and safety

- how to respond to contradictions between health and safety requirements and organisational constraints.

THE IMPORTANCE OF HEALTH AND SAFETY IN THE WORKPLACE

The achievement of the highest standards of health and safety in the workplace is important because:

- The elimination, or at least minimisation, of health and safety hazards and risks is the moral as well as the legal responsibility of employers – this is the overriding reason.

- Ill-health and injuries resulting from the system of work or from working conditions cause suffering and loss to individuals and their dependants.

- Accidents and absences through ill-health or injuries result in losses and damage to the organisation: this 'business' reason is much, much less significant than the 'human' reasons given above but remains a consideration, albeit a tangential one.

What importance is attached to health and safety matters in your organisation and for what reason? Is the level of importance satisfactory – and if not, why not?

LEGISLATIVE REQUIREMENTS

The Health and Safety at Work (etc) Act 1974

This Act sets out the basic duties of an employer:

- to install a safe working system
- to provide safe premises, a safe working environment and safe equipment
- to employ trained and competent people
- to give proper instruction and supervision to ensure that healthy and safe systems and conditions of work are achieved.

The duties of employers apply not only to their full-time workers but also to part-timers, trainees, casual workers and subcontractors. They apply to anyone allowed to use the employers' equipment or visit their premises, and extend to anyone affected by what the employer does – for example, neighbours or members of the public and those who use the products of the organisation or the services it provides.

Employers who employ five or more people are required to set out written statements of their health and safety policy and the arrangements they have in force to further the intentions of the policy. They have to consult with their employees on measures for promoting health and safety, which implies discussing the contents of the policy with them before it is published. Annual reports of companies registered under the Companies Act are required to include presented information about accidents and occupational diseases suffered by the company's employees and about preventive measures taken by the companies.

The Act additionally lays down that it is the duty of employees to observe the legal health and safety provisions and to act with due care for themselves and others.

What do you think are the most important messages this Act conveys to individual managers in a business?

REGULATIONS

A number of major regulations came into force during the 1990s. The six 1992 regulations – sometimes known as the 'six-pack' – were introduced to implement the European Framework Directive and its five associated directives in Great Britain.

The 'six-pack' regulations are:

- the *Management of Health and Safety at Work Regulations 1992* – These established a structured approach to the management of health and safety at work. They placed a specific legal duty on employers to carry out detailed risk assessments, as well as strengthening safety representatives' consultative rights.

- the *Health and Safety (Display Screen Equipment) Regulations* 1992 – These regulations provide for eye tests and training for regular users of display screen equipment.

- the *Manual Handling Operations Regulations* 1992 – These require employees to avoid hazardous manual handling operations wherever possible.

- the *Personal Protective Equipment at Work Regulations 1992* – These regulations set out comprehensive requirements on the provision of personal protective equipment.

- the *Protection and Use of Work Equipment Regulations* (PUWER)1992 – The selection, suitability and maintenance of all equipment in the workplace are covered in these regulations.

- the *Workplace (Health, Safety and Welfare) Regulations* 1992 – These regulations set out minimum standards for cleanliness, ventilation, temperature, lighting and maintenance.

In addition, the *Control of Substances Hazardous to Health* (COSHH) *Regulations* 1994 are designed to protect employees who work with dangerous substances.

What can and should an organisation do to ensure that these regulations are understood and applied?

What is the most significant point in the Management of Health and Safety at Work Regulations 1992, and what are its implications?

What can and should an organisation do to implement the Health and Safety (Display Screen Equipment) Regulations 1992?

CODES OF PRACTICE

Codes of Practice have been produced by the Health and Safety Executive (HSE) which are concerned with the implementation of the key regulations. They offer sound advice and information developed through the experience of the HSE field staff or gained from other professional bodies and organisations. They should be considered carefully when developing and introducing health and safety policies and procedures and when conducting risk assessments, safety audits and accident investigations.

Obtain a copy of a relevant HSE Code of Practice. To what extent do the practices of your organisation in this area conform to the code?

HEALTH AND SAFETY POLICIES

Written health and safety policies are required to demonstrate that top management is concerned about the protection of the organisation's employees from hazards at work and to indicate how this protection will be provided. Such written policies are, therefore, first a declaration of intent, second a definition of the means by which that intent will be realised, and third a statement of the guidelines which should be followed by everyone concerned – which means all employees – in implementing the policy.

The policy statement should consist of three parts:

- the overall statement of policy

- a description of the facilities and the personnel provided by the organisation for health and safety

- details of arrangements for implementing the policy by means of those facilities and personnel.

The overall policy statement

The overall policy statement should be a declaration of the intention of the employer to safeguard the health and safety of employees. It should emphasise four fundamental points:

- that the safety of employees and the public is of paramount importance

- that safety takes precedence over expediency

- that every effort will be made to involve all managers, team leaders and employees in the development and implementation of health and safety procedures

- that health and safety legislation will be complied with in the spirit as well as the letter of the law.

Organisation

This section of the policy statement should describe the health and safety arrangements of the company through which high standards are set and (hopefully) achieved by people at all levels in the organisation.

This section should underline the ultimate responsibility of top management for the health and safety performance of the organisation. It should then indicate how key management personnel may be held accountable for performance in their areas. The role of safety representatives and safety committees should be defined, and the duties of specialists such as the safety adviser and the medical officer should be summarised.

Why are health and safety policies important? What are the key messages they should convey?

CONDUCTING RISK ASSESSMENTS

Risk assessments are concerned with the identification of hazards and the analysis of the risks attached to them.

A *hazard* is anything that can cause harm (eg working on roofs, lifting heavy objects, potentially harmful chemicals, high-voltage electricity, etc). A *risk* is the chance, large or small, of harm's being actually caused by the hazard. Risk assessments are concerned with looking for hazards and estimating the level of risk associated with them. As suggested by Holt and Andrews,[1] risk can be calculated by multiplying a severity estimate by a probability estimate – that is,

$$\text{risk} = \text{severity} \times \text{probability}$$

The purpose of risk assessments is, of course, to initiate preventive action. They enable control measures to be devised on the basis of an understanding of the relative importance of risks. Risk assessments must by law be recorded if there are five or more employees.

There are two types of risk assessment. The first is *quantitative risk assessment*, which produces an objective probability estimate based upon risk information which is immediately applicable to the circumstances in which the risk occurs. The second is *qualitative risk assessment*, which is more subjective and is based on judgement backed by generalised data. Quantitative risk assessment is preferable if the specific data is available. Qualitative risk assessment may be acceptable if there is little or no specific data, as long as it is made systematically on the basis of an analysis of working conditions and hazards, and on an informed judgement of the likelihood of harm's actually being caused.

Looking for hazards
The following, as suggested by the HSE and others, are typical activities in which accidents happen or in association with which there are high risks:

- receipt of raw materials – eg involving lifting, carrying

- stacking and storage – eg where there may be falling materials

- movement of people and materials – eg potential falls, collisions

- processing of raw materials – eg possible exposure to toxic substances

- maintenance of buildings – eg while carring out roof-work, gutter-cleaning

- maintenance of plant and machinery – eg when lifting tackle, installing equipment

- using electricity – eg in using hand tools, setting up extension leads

- operating machines – eg if operating without sufficient clearance, or at an unsafe speed; if not using safety devices

- not wearing protective equipment – eg hats, boots, clothing

- distributing finished jobs – eg when delivering vehicles

- dealing with emergencies – eg spillages, fires, explosions

- using equipment or methods of working subject to intrinsic health hazards – eg VDUs, possible repetitive strain injuries from badly designed work stations or working practices.

The HSE suggests that most accidents are caused by a few key activities. It advises that assessors should concentrate initially on those that could cause serious harm. Operations such as roof-work, machine-maintenance and transport movement cause far more deaths and injuries each year than many mainstream activities.

When carrying out a risk assessment it is also necessary to consider who else might be harmed – eg employees, visitors (including cleaners and contractors and the public when calling in to buy products or enlist services).

> Consider a typical office. If you were carrying out a risk assessment, what hazards would you look for?

Hazards should be ranked according to their potential severity as a basis for reducing one side of the risk equation. A simple three-point scale can be used, such as 'low', 'moderate' and 'high'. A more complex severity-rating scale has been proposed by Holt and Andrews:[2]

- *catastrophic* – imminent danger exists: hazard capable of causing death and illness on a wide scale

- *critical* – hazard can result in serious illness, severe injury, damage to property and equipment

- *marginal* – hazard can cause illness, injury, or equipment damage, but the results would probably not be serious

- *negligible* – hazard should not result in serious injury or illness; the possibility of damage beyond requiring minor first-aid is remote.

Assessing the risk

When the hazards have been identified it is necessary to assess how high the risks are. The HSE suggests that this involves answering three questions:

- What would be the worst result?

- How likely is that to happen?

- How many people could be hurt if things go wrong?

A probability rating system can be used, such as the one recommended by Holt and Andrews:[3]

- *probable* – likely to occur immediately or shortly

- *reasonably probable* – probably will occur in time

- *remote* – may occur in time

- *extremely remote* – unlikely to occur.

> Carry out a hazard assessment for a typical office (see earlier question). How high are the risks of injury or threats to health arising from each of these hazards?

Taking action

Risk assessment should lead to action. The type of action to be taken can be ranked in order of potential effectiveness in the form of a 'safety precedence sequence' as proposed by Holt and Andrews:

- *hazard elimination* – use of alternatives, design improvements, change of process

- *substitution* – for example, replacement of one chemical substance with another that is less risky

- *use of barriers* – displacing the hazard from the worker or displacing the worker from the hazard

- *use of procedures* – limitation of exposure, dilution of exposure, safe systems of work (all these depend on human initiative)

- *use of warning systems* – signs, instructions, labels (all these also depend on human initiative)

- *use of personal protective clothing* – this depends on human response and is used as a side measure only when all other options have been exhausted.

> Refer to the office for which you have carried out a risk assessment. For each identified hazard – and taking into account the assessment of the risk of injury or illness – set out proposed actions with reference to the safety precedence sequence.

Monitoring and evaluation

Risk assessment is not completed when action against the risk has been initiated. It is essential to monitor the hazard and evaluate the effectiveness of the action in eliminating it or at least reducing it to an acceptable level.

What is a risk assessment?
What is a hazard?
What is the difference between quantitative and qualitative risk assessments? When might it be necessary to rely on the latter?
What systems of rating can be used to assess risks?
What is the safety precedence sequence?

HEALTH AND SAFETY AUDITS

Risk assessments identify specific hazards and quantify the risks attached to them. Health and safety audits provide for a much more comprehensive review of all aspects of health and safety policies and procedures and practices programmes. As defined by Saunders,[4]

> A safety audit will examine the whole organisation in order to test whether it is meeting its safety aims and objectives. It will examine hierarchies, safety-planning processes, decision-making, delegation, policy-making and implementation.

Who carries out a health and safety audit?

Safety audits can be conducted by safety advisers and/or personnel specialists, but the more managers, employees and trade union representatives are involved the better. Audits are often carried out under the auspices of a health and safety committee whose members take an active part in conducting them.

Managers can also be held responsible for conducting audits within their departments. Even better, individual members of these departments can be trained to carry out audits in particular areas. The conduct of an audit is made considerably easier if checklists are prepared and a simple form used to record results.

Some organisations also use outside agencies (such as the British Safety Institute) to conduct independent audits.

What is covered by a health and safety audit?

A health and safety audit should cover:

- *Policies*
  - Do health and safety policies meet legal requirements?
  - Are senior managers committed to health and safety?
  - How committed are other managers, team leaders and supervisors to health and safety?
  - Is there a health and safety committee? If not, why not?
  - How effective is the committee in getting things done?

- *Procedures* – How effectively do the procedures
  - support the implementation of health and safety policies?
  - communicate the need for good health and safety practices?
  - provide for systematic risk assessments?
  - ensure that accidents are investigated thoroughly?
  - record data on health and safety which is used to evaluate performance and initiate action?
  - ensure that health and safety considerations are given proper weight when designing systems of work or manufacturing and operational processes (including the design of equipment and work stations, the specification for the product or service, and the use of materials)?
  - provide safety training, especially induction training and training when jobs or working methods are changed?

- *Safety practices*
  - To what extent do health and safety practices in all areas of the organisation conform to the general requirements of the Health and Safety at Work Act and the specific requirements of the various regulations and Codes of Practice?
  - What risk assessments have been carried out? What were the findings? What actions were taken?
  - What is the health and safety performance of the organisation as shown by the performance indicators? Is the trend positive or negative? If negative, what is being done about it?

- How thoroughly are accidents investigated? What steps
  have been taken to prevent their recurrence?
- What is the evidence that managers and supervisors are
  really concerned about health and safety?

The audit should cover the questions above, but its
purpose is to generate action. Those conducting the audit
will have to assess priorities and costs and draw up action
programmes for approval by the board.

Example

An example of an auditing system is provided by Sharp
Manufacturing (source: IDS[5]). This consists of four tiers:

1 A number of employees are nominated by their
  departmental managers to carry out safety sampling in
  their own section at least every two weeks. The safety
  samplers, who have received training by their managers
  in hazard-spotting, work from a checklist of key elements
  of safety in their own particular workplace. Sampling
  consists of 10–15 spot-checks, looking at such things as
  housekeeping, protective clothing and any risky elements
  of working to establish a picture of accident potential and
  the changes needed.

2 Monthly inspections are carried out by trade union safety
  representatives, who use the same checklist to ensure
  high safety standards.

3 Every three months, safety tours are made throughout
  the plant by the safety manager and the personnel
  manager together with representatives of the area being
  audited.

4 A formal audit of Sharp's safety systems is carried out
  every year by an outside agency. The British Safety
  Council undertakes a five-star health and safety
  management audit which examines 77 key elements in
  five areas of safety, ranging from safety organisations and
  housekeeping to machinery and personal safeguarding.
  (Sharp has on a number of occasions won a five-star
  award which requires a minimum of a 91 per cent rating
  by the British Safety Council.)

What is the difference between a health and safety audit and a risk assessment?
How would you recommend that a health and safety audit should be carried out in your organisation?
What are the main aspects of health and safety that should be covered by an audit?

SAFETY INSPECTIONS

Safety inspections are intended to examine a specific area of the organisation – an operational department or a manufacturing process – in order to locate and define any faults in the system, equipment, plant or machines, or any operational errors that might be the source of accidents. Safety inspections should be carried out on a regular and systematic basis by line managers and supervisors with the advice and help of health and safety advisers. The steps to be taken in carrying out safety inspections are:

- Allocate the responsibility for conducting the inspection to a specific individual.

- Define the points to be covered in the form of a checklist.

- Divide the department or plant into areas and list the points to which attention needs to be given in each area.

- Use the checklists as the basis for the inspection.

- Define the frequency with which inspections should be carried out – daily in critical areas.

- Carry out sample- or spot-checks on a random basis.

- Carry out special investigations as necessary to deal with special problems such as operating machinery without guards to increase throughput.

- Set up a reporting system (a form should be used for recording the results of inspections).

- Set up a system for monitoring safety inspections to

ensure they are being conducted properly and on schedule, and that corrective action has been taken where necessary.

> What is the purpose of a safety inspection?
> What items might be covered by an inspection?
> Who should be responsible for conducting inspections?

ACCIDENT PREVENTION

The prevention of accidents is achieved by

- identifying the previous and likely causes of accidents and the conditions under which they occur

- taking account of safety factors at the design stage – building safety into the system

- designing safety equipment and protective devices and providing protective clothing

- carrying out regular risk assessments, audits, inspections and checks, and taking action to eliminate risks

- investigating all accidents that result in damage to establish the cause and to initiate corrective action

- maintaining good records and statistics in order to identify problem areas and unsatisfactory trends

- conducting a continuous programme of education and training on safe working habits and methods of avoiding accidents

- leadership and motivation – encouraging methods of leadership and motivation which do not place excessive demands on people.

> What steps can an organisation take to prevent accidents?
> What is meant when reference is made to the 'system of work' as a major cause of accidents?
> Consider an accident at work (however minor) which you have experienced yourself or have first-hand knowledge of. How would you have investigated it? What were the causes? What recommendations would you make to prevent a recurrence?

MEASURING HEALTH AND SAFETY PERFORMANCE

The saying that 'If you can't measure it, you can't manage it' is totally applicable to health and safety. It is essential to know what is happening; it is even more essential to measure trends as a means of identifying in good time where actions are necessary.

The most common measures are:

- *the frequency rate*

$$\frac{\text{number of injuries} \times 100,000}{\text{number of hours worked}}$$

- *the incidence rate*

$$\frac{\text{number of injuries} \times 1,000}{\text{average number employed during the period}}$$

- *the severity rate* – the days lost through accidents or occupation health problems per 1,000,000 hours worked.

Some organisations adopt a 'total loss control' approach which covers the cost of accidents to the business under such headings as 'pay to people off work', 'damage to plant or equipment' and 'loss of production'. A cost severity rate can then be calculated, which is the total cost of accident per 1,000,000 hours worked.

COMMUNICATING THE NEED FOR BETTER HEALTH AND SAFETY PRACTICES

As Holt and Andrews[6] observe, various forms of propaganda to sell the health and safety message have been used for many years, although 'They are now widely felt to be of little value in measurable terms in changing behaviour and influencing attitudes to health and safety issues.' But they believe that it is still necessary to deliver the message that health and safety is important as long as this supplements rather than replaces other initiatives. They suggest (pp. 103–114) that specific steps can be taken to increase the effectiveness of safety messages:

- *avoid negatives* – Successful safety propaganda should contain positive messages, not warnings of the unpleasant consequences of actions.

- *expose correctly* – Address the message to the right people at the point of danger.

- *use attention-getting techniques carefully* – Lurid images may only be remembered for what they are, not for the message they are trying to convey.

- *maximise comprehension* – Messages should be simple and specific.

- *messages must be believable* – They should address real issues and be perceived as being delivered by people (ie managers) who believe in what they say and are doing something about it.

- *messages must point the way to action* – The most effective messages call for positive actions which can be achieved by the receivers and will offer them a tangible benefit.

Approaches to briefing staff on the importance of health and safety

Advice to a group of staff on the importance of health and safety in the workplace must be based on a thorough understanding of the organisation's health and safety policies and procedures and an appreciation of the particular factors affecting the health and safety of the group of people concerned. Identification of those particular factors can be based on information provided by risk assessments, safety audits and accident reports. But the advice must be positive – why health and safety is important and how accidents can be prevented. The advice should not be over-weighted by awful warnings.

The points to be made include:

- a review of the health and safety policies of the organisation, with explanations of the reasoning behind them and a positive statement of management's belief that health and safety is a major consideration because

1) it directly affects the well-being of all concerned, and
2) it can, and does, minimise suffering and loss

- a review of the procedures used by the organisation for the business as a whole and in the area concerned an assessment of the risks and audit safety situation

- an explanation of the roles of the members of the group in carrying out their work safely and giving full consideration to the safety of others

- a reiteration of the statement that one of the core values of the organisation is the maintenance of safe systems of work and the promotion of safe working practices.

You are asked to prepare a presentation to a group of staff in your organisation on the importance of health and safety. How would you tackle it?

You have been asked by your manager to make recommendations on what form a health and safety communication programme addressed both to shop floor and office workers should take. What recommendations would you propose?

HEALTH AND SAFETY TRAINING

Health and safety training is a key part of the preventive programme. It should start as part of the induction course. It should also take place following a transfer to a new job or a change in working methods. Safety training spells out the rules and provides information on potential hazards and how to avoid them. Further refresher training should be provided and special courses laid on to deal with new aspects of health and safety or areas in which safety problems have emerged.

An example of safety training

As reported by IDS, Leyland Trucks provide Leyland employees with a minimum of thirty-seven-and-a-half hours' training every year, with a sizeable chunk devoted to health and safety. In addition, operators receive extra health and safety training based on an analysis of needs.

Under the company's system of 'toolbox' training, 30 modules are available on safety. This allows weekly sessions to be run by the business unit manager, as part of a 'quality hour' when the trucks are stopped. Around half the time is devoted to safety.

Immediate response training is organised after any incident judged to need action. Managers receive refresher training as do shop stewards who are safety representatives.

> What are the key points you would make in the introductory session of an induction programme?

ORGANISING HEALTH AND SAFETY

Health and safety concerns everyone in an establishment, although the main responsibility lies with management in general and individual managers in particular. The specific roles are summarised below.

Management develops and implements health and safety policies and ensures that procedures for carrying out risk assessments, safety audits and inspections are implemented. Importantly, management has the duty of monitoring and evaluating health and safety performance and taking corrective action as necessary.

Managers can exert the greater influence on health and safety. They are in immediate control and it is up to them to keep a constant watch for unsafe conditions or practices and to take immediate action. They are also directly responsible for ensuring that employees are conscious of health and safety hazards and do not take risks.

Employees should be aware of what constitutes safe working practices as they affect them and their fellow-workers. Whereas management and managers have the duty to communicate and train, individuals also have the duty to take account of what they have heard and learned in the ways they carry out their work.

Health and safety advisers advise on policies and procedures and on healthy and safe methods of working. They conduct risk assessments and safety audits and investigations into accidents in conjunction with managers and health and safety representatives, they maintain statistics, and they report on trends and necessary actions.

Medical advisers have two functions: preventive and clinical. The preventive function is most important, especially on occupational health matters. The clinical function is to deal with industrial accidents and diseases and to advise on the steps necessary to recover from injury or illness arising from work. They do not usurp the role of the family doctor in non-work-related illnesses.

Safety committees consisting of health and safety representatives advise on health and safety policies and procedures, help in conducting risk assessments and safety audits, and make suggestions on improving health and safety performance.

CONTRADICTIONS

Contradictions may arise between health and safety priorities and organisational constraints. The only response to such contradictions is to attach priority always to health and safety considerations. Operational necessity (real or assumed) is no excuse for cutting corners. Some work carried out in organisations may be inherently dangerous to a certain extent, but the dangers must be recognised and work should be allowed on these operations only when every possible precaution has been taken against accidents by developing a safe system of work and by other preventive measures, including training. It is also inevitable that some work may involve the use of dangerous substances, but such substances must be isolated from the worker or the worker isolated from them. Proper training and supervision is particularly necessary in these circumstances.

> What should be the key features of an organisation's health and safety procedures?
> How would you advise a specified group of staff on the importance of health and safety in the workplace?
> Why is it important to create and maintain a safe and healthy workplace environment?
> What are the key headings you would expect to find in a health and safety policy?
> What are the distinctions between the purposes of risk assessments, of health and safety audits and of safety inspections?

OCCUPATIONAL HEALTH PROGRAMMES

The Health and Safety Executive reported in 1998 that almost 20 million working days a year are lost because of work-related illness. Two million people say they suffer from an illness they believe was caused by their work. Muscular disorders, including repetitive strain injury and back pain, are by far the most commonly reported illnesses with 1.2 million affected, and the numbers are rising. The next biggest problem is stress, which 500,000 people say is so bad that it is making them ill. These are large and disturbing figures, and they show that high priority must be given to creating and maintaining programmes for the improvement of occupational health.

The control of occupational health and hygiene problems can be achieved by

* eliminating hazards at source through design and process engineering

* isolating hazardous processes and substances so that workers do not come into contact with them

* changing the processes or substances used to promote better protection or eliminate the risk

* providing protective equipment – but only if changes to the design, process or specification cannot completely remove the hazard

- training workers to avoid risk

- maintaining plant and equipment to eliminate the possibility of harmful emissions, controlling the use of toxic substances, and eliminating radiation hazards

- good housekeeping to keep premises and machinery clean and free from toxic substances

- regular inspections to ensure that potential health risks are identified in good time

- pre-employment medical examinations and regular checks on those exposed to risk

- ensuring that ergonomic considerations (ie the design and use of equipment, machines, processes and workstations) are taken into account in design specifications, establishing work routines and training – this is particularly important as a means of minimising the incidence of repetitive strain injury (RSI)

- maintaining preventive medicine programmes which develop health standards for each job and involve regular audits of potential health hazards and regular examinations for anyone at risk.

Particular attention needs to be exercised on the control of noise, fatigue and stress. Control of stress should be regarded as a major part of any occupational health programme.

Managing stress

There are four main reasons why organisations should take account of stress and do something about it – first, because they have the social responsibility to provide a good quality of working life; second, because excessive stress causes illness; third, because it can result in inability to cope with the demands of the job which, of course, creates more stress; and finally, because excessive stress can reduce employee effectiveness and therefore organisational performance.

The ways in which stress can be managed by an organisation include:

- *job design* – clarifying roles, reducing the danger of role ambiguity and conflict and giving people more autonomy within a defined structure to manage their responsibilities

- *targets and performance standards* – setting reasonable and achievable targets which may stretch people but do not place impossible burdens on them

- *placement* – taking care to place people in jobs which are within their capabilities

- *career development* – planning careers and promoting staff in accordance with their capabilities, taking care not to over- or under-promote

- *performance-management processes* – allowing a dialogue to take place between managers and individuals about the individuals' work problems and ambitions

- *counselling* – giving individuals the opportunity to talk about their problems with a member of the personnel department or the company medical officer, or through an employee-assistance programme

- *management training* – training in performance review and counselling techniques and in what managers can do to alleviate their own stress and reduce it in others.

In a mail-order company absence rates through illness have been increasing for key punch operators (who are expected to meet demanding targets for key depressions per hour). You have been asked to investigate the causes.

- How would you conduct the investigation?
- What causes might you possibly identify?
- What action would you recommend?

Consider your own job or any other job with which you are familiar. To what extent is it stressful, and what could the organisation do about it?

SUMMARY

- Health and safety management is vital: a systematic and concerted effort is needed to minimise suffering and loss from accidents and occupational health problems.

- A powerful legislative framework of health and safety regulations is in place, supported by Codes of Practice, and founded on the overarching Health and Safety at Work (etc) Act, 1974.

- Risk assessment identifies hazards, estimates their severity and determines the likelihood or probability of the hazards leading to accidents. The degree of risk can be expressed in the formula *severity* $\times$ *probability*. Risk assessment leads to action which must be monitored and evaluated.

- Health and safety audits provide for a comprehensive review of all safety policies, procedures and practices to ensure that they meet health and safety aims and objectives.

- Safety inspections examine a specific area or process to locate any constituent elements in the system of work which might be the source of accidents so that corrective action can be taken.

- Occupational health programmes aim to deal with health hazards at source, by changing or isolating hazardous substances or processes, by setting up regular inspections, and by attending to ergonomic considerations in the design of work processes and stations.

- Accident prevention programmes identify the causes of potential accidents (primarily factors within systems of work), ensure that safety is built into the system, and monitor the design of safety equipment and protective devices.

- Health and safety performance indicators are used to identify trends in the frequency and severity of accidents or absence through work-related illness so that corrective action can be taken.

• Training in safety procedures is essential, especially for new starters and when jobs or processes are changed.

REFERENCES

1 HOLT A. *and* ANDREWS H. *Principles of Health and Safety at Work*. London, IOSH Publishing, 1993.

2 HOLT *and* ANDREWS, see Note 1 above.

3 HOLT *and* ANDREWS, see Note 1 above.

4 SAUNDERS R. *The Safety Audit*. London, Pitman, 1992.

5 IDS Study. *Safety at Work*. London, Incomes Data Services, March 1997.

6 HOLT *and* ANDREWS, see Note 1 above.

Part 3

QUALITY AND CONTINUOUS IMPROVEMENT

13 Managing and achieving quality

Quality can be defined as the degree of excellence achieved by an organisation in delivering products or services to its customers. There are three aspects of quality:

- *quality of design* – the degree to which the design achieves its purpose

- *quality of conformance* – the extent to which the product conforms with the design specification

- *quality of customer satisfaction* – the level at which value is delivered to customers by satisfying their needs.

Of these three aspects, the last is by far the most important. Quality of design and quality of conformance serve the sole purpose of satisfying customers. Quality is essentially a customer-oriented concept. Customer satisfaction is obtained by product designs or service programmes which meet their needs, by achieving quality specifications which have been built into the design of the product or service, by attaining high standards of reliability and equally high levels of customer service, and by paying constant attention to customer care.

The level of quality reached by an organisation is thus measured in terms of the extent to which customer requirements are satisfied. However, the reputation of an organisation for quality products or services extends beyond individual customers to the community at large. And this reputation must be protected and enhanced.

Competitive advantage is achieved by businesses which provide goods or services to quality levels higher than those offered by competitors. But they will be striving equally hard to match or exceed those levels. This means that policies of continuous improvement have to be implemented to maintain competitive advantage. Quality is a race without a finish: it is a race against tough competitors to achieve and sustain world-class performance. Quality differentiates companies from these competitors.

Quality management

Quality has to be managed. It is not achieved easily. And it cannot be left to chance. Everyone in an organisation has to play their part, but what they do must be planned, monitored, measured and controlled. In short, they have to be managed.

There are a number of approaches to managing quality as defined later in this chapter. The overarching concept is that of 'total quality', which is achieved when the quality of a product or service achieves customer satisfaction. This is often called 'total quality management' (TQM) – but quality can be managed well without calling it TQM, and this chapter is concerned with *all* aspects of managing quality, not just TQM.

On completing it, a reader will understand:

- the various terms used in quality management – 'quality assurance', 'quality control', 'inspection', 'statistical quality control', 'total quality', 'total quality control', 'total quality management', etc

- the contribution of the quality 'gurus' Deming, Juran and Crosby

- the quality standards available: 1S0 9000 as based on BS 5750, and the EFQM model

- the basic principles of quality management

- the development and implementation of quality management programmes

- how to measure and monitor quality

- who is responsible for quality

- the processes of empowering and involving people to achieve quality.

The important subjects of continuous improvement and customer care are treated separately in the next two chapters.

Give three reasons why you think effective quality management is important in an organisation.

QUALITY ASSURANCE AND QUALITY CONTROL

Quality assurance

Quality assurance involves the use of documented procedures designed to ensure that the activities carried out in the organisation (design, development, manufacturing, service delivery) result in products or services which meet the requirements and needs of customers. The underpinning philosophy of quality assurance is that right methods will produce right results (quality products or services).

Quality control

Quality control involves the application of data collection and analysis to monitor and measure the extent to which quality assurance requirements have been met in terms of product or service performance and reliability. The traditional approach to controlling quality is inspection. Control can be exercised more scientifically by means of statistical techniques. When control is applied systematically throughout an organisation it is referred to as total quality control. These approaches to monitoring quality are described below.

Inspection

Inspection is an after-the-event activity concerned with

locating faults when they have already occurred so that they can be put right. Ideally, quality assurance and control procedures should eliminate the need for inspection. But we do not live in an ideal world and inspection procedures are still used in many manufacturing organisations as the final safety-net.

Statistical quality control

Statistical quality control uses sampling techniques and mathematical analysis to ensure that during design, manufacturing and servicing, work is carried out and material used within the specified limits required to produce the desired standards of quality, performance and reliability. The aim is to minimise defects, not only for the practical reason that defects lose business but also because, ethically, no self-respecting company deserves to survive on the sale of sub-standard products or the delivery of inferior services. But the approach to the reduction of defects must consider the cost of their minimisation, and statistical quality control techniques identify not only the scope for improvement but also the cost of achieving the desired result.

The main techniques used in statistical quality control are:

- *acceptance sampling* – which ensures that items do not pass to the next stage in the process if an unacceptably high proportion of the batch is outside the quality limit. Sampling consists of taking a representative number of examples from a population and drawing conclusions about the behaviour of the whole population from the behaviour of the sample. Sampling techniques are based on statistical theory, including probability theory.

- *control charts* – on which the results of the inspection of samples are compared with the results expected from a stable situation. If they do not match, action may be necessary. These comparisons can be recorded graphically on control charts on which warning and action levels are marked. Control charts set out the control limits which either warn that a problem exists or indicate that action needs to be taken (warning and action limits).

- *control by attributes* – attributes have only two states – whether an article or service is acceptable or not. The information required for control purposes compares the number of defects and/or the number of defects per unit, which are compared with the desired level of quality – the acceptable quality level (AQL).

- *control by variables* – variables can have any value on a continuous scale. Control by variables therefore takes place when a distribution of features is being measured rather than where there is a go or no-go position as in control by attributes. Variables are therefore measured, in contrast to attributes, which are counted.

Total quality control

Total quality control processes aim to organise quality into the product or service by pursuing policies of assuring and controlling quality. The emphasis is on the prevention of quality problems before the event, rather than on dealing with them after the event through inspections. Statistical control techniques may be used but they are only part of the total process. Total quality control takes a comprehensive view of all aspects of quality through techniques such as zero-defects programmes or Taguchi methodology.

Zero-defects programmes

Zero-defects programmes aim to improve product quality beyond the level that might economically be achieved through statistical procedures. The ultimate aim is to eliminate defects so far as is conceivably possible.

The principal features of such programmes are:

- Agreement is reached with all concerned over the quality goals to be attained and the quality problems which might prevent their achievement.

- The participation of all those involved in establishing and running the quality programme is organised.

- Clear targets are set against which improvements can be measured.

- Procedures are established for providing prompt feedback to employees on their quality achievements.

- Rewards are offered for achieving high quality standards.

- Employees are encouraged to make suggestions on the causes of errors and the remedies, and ideas are then implemented jointly.

- Work is organised and jobs are designed to facilitate all of the above.

Taguchi methodology

This methodology was developed by the Japanese engineer Taguchi. Its main features are to

- push quality back to the design stage because quality control can never compensate for bad design

- emphasise design rather than inspection for control of production

- produce robust products with intrinsic quality and reliability characteristics

- prototype product designs and production processes

- concentrate on the practical engineering, not the statistical niceties of quality control theory.

Evaluate the main features and merits of monitoring quality control as set out in the three approaches described above: inspection, statistical quality control, and total quality control.

TOTAL QUALITY

Total quality is an overarching concept which embraces everything an organisation does to deliver value and high levels of satisfaction to its customers. Total quality implies the use of a disciplined, structured and all-embracing approach to quality management. It incorporates quality assurance and quality control techniques but, as the name implies, it includes all aspects of an organisation's activities and concerns everyone in the organisation. It is thus focused on delivering quality services to internal as well as external customers.

The four basic principles of total quality are:

- *Customer satisfaction* – The only real measure of the quality of a product or service is the extent to which it delivers customer satisfaction. The word 'satisfaction' can be defined as when all customers' wants, needs and expectations are met, whether or not they have been verbally expressed and whether or not any feedback is forthcoming.

- *Continuous improvement* – The concept of continuous improvement is based on the belief that continually striving to reach higher and higher standards in every part of the organisation will result in a series of incremental gains that will engender superior performance. It involves creating an environment in which *all* employees contribute to improving performance and quality as a normal part of their job.

- *The significance of internal customers* – This relies on the concept that everyone who receives goods or services from a colleague within an organisation is a customer of that colleague. Suppliers of goods and services within an organisation have to be just as aware of the need to achieve high levels of quality for their colleagues as for their ultimate customers. The ultimate goal of complete customer satisfaction can only be guaranteed if attention is paid to quality in all the transactions and processes which take place within the organisation.

- *An all-embracing approach* – The concept of total quality focuses on the requirement for *all* employees in the organisation to be involved *all* the time in meeting *all* customer requirements.

The concept of total quality incorporates the notion of total quality control but goes even further in emphasising that quality should be managed into the system, and that quality management should always be oriented towards the achievement of complete customer satisfaction.

A total quality approach is a systematic way of ensuring that all activities within an organisation happen exactly as they have been planned in order to meet the defined needs of customers. The emphasis is on involving everyone in the organisation in activities which provide for continuous improvement and for achieving sustained high levels of performance.

The philosophy is about getting commitment to quality. Everyone at every level in the organisation has genuinely to believe in quality and to act on that belief. Total quality can be described as an attitude of mind which leads to appropriate behaviour and actions. It has to be, as at Nissan, the centre-piece of the company's philosophy, with commitment at *every level* to a zero-defect product.

> Distinguish the particular characteristics of total quality from those of quality assurance and quality control processes.

Total quality management

Total quality management (TQM) can be defined as a systematic way of guaranteeing that all activities within an organisation happen exactly as they have been planned in order to meet the defined needs of customers. Put like this it seems conceptually to be the same as total quality, the philosophy of which it essentially shares. TQM could be regarded as a method of systematising or packaging the notion of total quality so that it can act as a brand name which managements can identify with when introducing quality programmes. However, Hutchins[1] suggests that TQM is a sub-set of total quality. In his opinion, the word *management* means 'authoritative control over the affairs of others': its addition to the concept of total quality is unhelpful and 'does nothing to encourage the cascade of quality responsibility down through the workforce'. This may be an extreme view which many TQM consultants would reject. They would claim that TQM *is* designed to encourage commitment to quality throughout the organisation and is not a top-down approach as Hutchins implies. TQM programmes can and generally do incorporate the principles of total quality as described above. But many organisations prefer to believe that what they are doing is managing total quality rather than TQM because TQM has in some quarters acquired the perhaps unjustified reputation of a management package or finite programme which, when introduced, solves every quality problem.

The rest of this chapter therefore describes approaches to total quality generally rather than focusing on the TQM brand of managing quality.

THE CONTRIBUTION OF THE QUALITY GURUS

Much of the thinking behind total quality was based on the work of the three principal quality gurus: Deming, Juran and Crosby.

W. Edwards Deming

Deming's[2] greatest contribution – which was based on his work in Japan – was to emphasise the importance of customers, the significance of continuous improvement, and the fact that quality is determined by the system.

He believed that competitiveness depends upon customer satisfaction which is created by a combination of responsiveness to customers' views and needs, and the continuous improvement of products or services. Furthermore, in order to remain competitive, organisations must constantly seek ways of improving their operational systems and the customer appeal of their products or services. Improvement is not just the responsibility of operations and sales departments, it must be the aim in all areas of the organisation and at all levels. And it must be a major influence on short-, medium- and long-term plans. Finally, the system determines quality levels. It is defined as inputs and the manner in which they are processed.

Deming's model of the quality cycle is illustrated in Figure 8.

Figure 8 The quality cycle

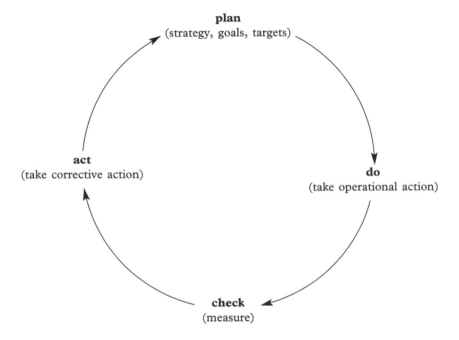

As described by Collard[3], Deming's quality model looks like Figure 9.

Figure 9 Deming's quality-centred model

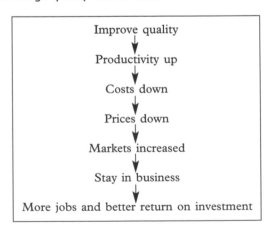

J. M. Juran

Juran's[4] major contribution to the philosophy of total quality was his concept of managerial breakthrough. In the traditional control situation, the typical managerial attitude is that the present level of performance is good enough or cannot be improved. The aim is therefore to perpetuate performance at that level. Management attempts simply to identify and eliminate short-term deviations from the usual performance.

Juran stated that in the breakthrough situation management adopts a completely different attitude. The belief is held strongly that change is desirable and possible in all aspects of operation. It is up to managers to make the 'breakthrough'. They must recognise and act on the need for what is, in effect, continuous improvement.

However, as Collard[5] points out,

> One of the difficulties, of course, is that managers simply have no time for 'breakthrough', because they cannot leave the treadmill of control. Few managers would argue against the merits of 'breakthrough', but they do need respite from the never-ending emergencies and crises. Seldom are harassed managers able to work their way out without help from top management and assistance from other specialists.

Philip B. Crosby

Crosby[6] emphasised that 'in discussing quality we are dealing with a people situation'. He suggested five factors which govern the management of quality:

- Quality means conformance, not elegance.

- There is no such thing as a quality problem.

- There is no such thing as the economics of quality. It is always cheaper to do the job right first time.

- The only performance measurement is the cost of quality.

- The only performance standard is zero defects.

> Deming said that organisations should eliminate the annual rating or merit system of performance appraisal because it is the organisation system, not the person, that counts. What do you think he meant by that? And to what extent do you agree? Collard commented that Juran's 'breakthrough' concept was difficult to apply in practice because managers were too focused on day-to-day problems. Explain what you think the significance of 'breakthrough' is. How can managers be placed in a position where they can make 'breakthroughs'?
> Crosby advocated and popularised the 'zero-defects' approach. What does this mean in practice? How realistic is it to aim for 'zero defects'?

QUALITY STANDARDS

Quality standards provide a set of principles – a template or framework which provides the basis for developing and measuring the effectiveness of a quality system. In effect, quality standards provide a specification for the capability of a business to manage quality. The first UK standard was BS 5750. This largely formed the basis for the international standard ISO 9000 which is the one most generally accepted. A further important development in quality standards has been produced by the European Foundation for Quality Management, the EFQM model.

BS 5750

BS (British Standard) 5750 provided the basis for ISO 9000. As an international standard it has become recognised as the most relevant one for British manufacturers, especially those trading abroad. The main provisions of BS 5750 which are largely incorporated in ISO 9000 are:

• A senior manager with the necessary authority must be clearly responsible for quality, with the task of co-ordinating and monitoring the quality system and seeing that prompt and effective action is taken to meet the standards.

• The nature and degree of organisation, structure,

resources, responsibilities, procedures and processes affecting quality must be documented.

- The quality system must be planned and developed to take account of all other functions such as customer liaison, manufacturing, purchasing, subcontracting, training and installation.

- Quality planning must identify the need for updating quality control techniques, ensuring that there is equipment and personnel capable of carrying out plans and providing for adequate quality records.

- There must be carefully documented control of design and development planning, with assignment of activities to qualified staff with adequate resources, control of interfaces between different disciplines and organisations, and documentation of design input requirements and design output.

- A co-ordinated system should be established which will ensure the provision of all appropriate documents covering planning, design, packaging, manufacture and inspection of products, as well as procedures which describe how functions shall be controlled, and where and when control should be exercised.

- Control in writing should be provided for purchased products and services, purchasing data, inspection and verification of purchased products, and the quality system to be applied (as appropriate) by the suppliers.

- Procedures and work instructions, including all customer specifications, should be defined in a simple form which covers every phase of manufacture, assembly and installation.

- Procedures should be set up for inspection and tests to be performed on incoming goods, taking account of the documented evidence of conformance provided with the goods.

- Procedures and records covering the control, calibration

and inspection of measuring and test equipment should be defined.

• Written control procedures should be defined in order to establish quickly at all times whether a product has been inspected.

• Systems for prompt and effective corrective action should be set up where non-conformance has been found.

• Written instructions and procedures should exist documenting the way a product is handled, stored and protected in the process and as it moves through the plant.

• Detailed records are required to show that customer quality requirements are being met, including data such as audit reports on the quality assurance system, results of inspections and tests, the calibration of test and measuring equipment, and corrective action taken.

• Effective internal quality audit systems should be set up and monitored by management.

• Provision of training, and records of training and of achievements of competence are necessary.

• Clear statistical procedures for monitoring quality standards should exist.

ISO 9000

ISO 9000 is the international standard for quality assurance. It provides a set of standards which are based on the same principles as those contained in BS 5750. However, it incorporates a more positive statement to the effect that the concept of quality underlying the standard is of meeting requirements. A product or service has quality when it satisfies the needs of users – customers. ISO 9000 is itself a statement about how quality is managed. It is a discipline for developing and implementing quality systems, and leads to certification if these standards are met. There are a number of related standards for particular operations – for example ISO 9002, which is concerned with quality in manufacturing.

In a sense, ISO 9000 defines quality in terms of conformance to requirements, while the total quality approach defines it as that which delights customers.

ISO 9000 provides a starting-point – a framework for developing quality control systems and a standard against which those systems can be assessed. But it is not a substitute for total quality with its emphasis on continuous improvement and involving everyone.

The EFQM model of quality

The European Foundation for Quality Management (EFQM) model as shown in Figure 10 indicates that customer satisfaction, people (employee) satisfaction and impact on society are achieved through leadership. Leadership drives the policy and strategy, the people management, resources and processes required to produce excellence in business results.

The EFQM model provides a much more dynamic set of standards for developing and measuring the effectiveness of total quality approaches than ISO 9000. The emphasis is on people and customers as well as processes.

Figure 10 The EFQM model

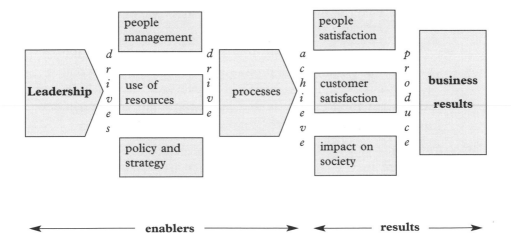

> Compare and contrast the approach adopted by ISO 9000 and EFQM quality standards. What have they each got to offer organisations? Is one potentially more valuable than the other? If so, why?

THE PRINCIPLES OF QUALITY MANAGEMENT

Quality management principles are based on the philosophy of total quality. They can be summed up in the terms 'customer satisfaction', 'continuous improvement', 'involving everyone', 'creating commitment to quality' and 'looking at the system as a whole'. This approach provides for the effective management of the dynamic relationship between what organisations have to do to develop and sustain customer satisfaction and the ever-changing needs of consumers and the continuous pressure of competition. It is a means of ensuring that quality is achieved and improved but does not obviate the need for quality control. Achievements must be measured to ensure that corrective action can be taken, and this action must focus on the root causes of the problem, not the symptoms.

The basic principles

The six basic principles of total quality as defined by Collard[7] are:

1 *Top management commitment* – Top management should continuously reinforce a total quality programme by what they do. They have to ensure that everyone knows how important total quality is and appreciates the long-term goals of the organisation's total quality processes.

2 *Attitude change* – Total quality requires a complete change in the attitude and culture prevailing in an organisation.

3 *Continuous improvement* – The need to create a climate of continuous improvement is linked to attitude change.

As Collard states, 'Quality improvement should always be at the forefront of *everything* that is done.'

4 *Supervision* – The successful introduction of total quality gives a key role to supervision in ensuring that the quality message is carried down to grassroots level.

5 *Training* – If the key to success is supervision, then it is important to ensure that the selection, training and motivation of supervisors allows for the development of the skills that enable them to become a dynamic force for improving performance.

6 *Recognition* – Performance and achievement in improving quality should be recognised. The recognition of contribution can be made effectively through non-financial means – publicly for individual or team achievement, competitions and prizes for teams.

> Consider your own organisation or any organisation you know and analyse the extent to which Collard's six principles have been applied. If they have been applied completely, or to a degree, what impact have they made on quality performance? You have been asked by your managing director to explain the foundation upon which a total quality approach should be adopted in your organisation. How would you use Collard's six principles in making your proposals?

THE DEVELOPMENT AND IMPLEMENTATION OF QUALITY MANAGEMENT PROCESSES

Quality management is a *process*, a way of doing things. It is not a programme with a finite start and finish. The management of quality is a continuous process which may make use of a number of techniques – for example, statistical quality control – but it ultimately depends on the attitudes and behaviour of all concerned. Quality management has to be based on a clearly stated policy.

Total quality policy
The policy could include the following points:

- The goal of the organisation is to achieve customer satisfaction by meeting the requirements of both external and internal customers.

- The need is to establish customer requirements and to respond quickly and effectively to them.

- It is essential to concentrate on prevention rather than cure.

- Everyone is involved – all work done by company employees, suppliers and product outlets is part of a process which creates a product or service for a customer.

- Each employee is a customer for work done by other employees and has the right to expect good work from them and the obligation to contribute work of high calibre to them.

- The standard of quality is 'zero defects' or 'no failures' – everyone has to understand the standards required and the need to do it right first time.

- Sustained quality excellence requires continuous improvement.

- Quality performance and costs should be measured systematically.

- Continuous attention must be paid to satisfying educational and training needs.

- High-quality performance will be recognised and rewarded.

- Quality improvement is best achieved by the joint efforts of all stakeholders.

Planning for total quality

Planning for total quality involves:

- recording the series of events and activities that constitute the total process by flow-charting and other means of activity analysis

- analysing the existing processes and system flows to establish inconsistencies and potential sources of variations and defects

- specifying for each activity the necessary quality-related activities, including material and packaging specifications, quality control procedures, process control systems, and sampling and inspection procedures

- developing, as appropriate, just-in-time (JIT) systems which provide for the right quantities to be produced or delivered at the right time and which ensure that there is no waste

- determining how to achieve quality in the purchasing system, with particular reference to the development of long-term relationships with suppliers so that dependable product quality and delivery standards can be defined and maintained

- conducting failure mode, effect and criticality (FMEC) studies to determine possible modes of failure and their effects on the performance of the product or service, and to establish which features of product design, production or operation are critical to the various modes of failure

- developing planned maintenance systems to reduce the incidence of emergency maintenance

- designing quality into the product, making sure that standards and specifications meet customer needs and can be achieved by existing processes (or, if not, by improving these processes in particular ways).

- conducting process capability studies to ensure that it will be possible to achieve quality standards through existing processes or, if not, to ascertain what changes are required

- examining quality requirements in manufacturing to ensure that answers can be forthcoming to the following questions: Can we make it? Are we making it? Have we made it? Could we make it better?

- studying storage, distribution and delivery arrangements to ensure that they are capable of meeting customer demands

- examining after-sales service procedures and achievements to identify areas for improvement.

What do you think are the most important actions an organisation should take when introducing total quality?

MEASURING AND MONITORING QUALITY

The process of managing quality as set out above aims to ensure that everyone is involved and committed to the continuous improvement of quality standards and to 'delighting' customers. But it is necessary to be explicit about the standards of quality required even if these are subject to continuous development. And it is equally important to measure and monitor quality performance against these standards. Only by doing this is it possible to identify where corrective action, aimed at the root causes of the problem, is required. Continuous improvement means doing everything better all the time, but it also means learning from problems and mistakes to ensure that they do not happen again. And this should be double- as well as single-loop learning – ie it is not a matter of simply correcting errors, it is much more about learning something new about what has to be achieved in the light of the changed circumstances and then deciding how it *can* be achieved. The emphasis is on using control information to initiate preventive as well as corrective action. In other words, it is not just about putting things right; it is truly about ensuring that things do not go wrong again.

The measurement and monitoring of quality can be carried out:

- at the most basic level, by simply comparing outputs or actions against predetermined standards

- by inspection – an after-the-event technique which does not address any real quality problems
- by the various techniques of statistical quality control – acceptance sampling, control charts, control by attributes, control by variables
- by statistical process control
- by benchmarking
- by customer and internal surveys.

Comparison of outputs and actions against standards

If standards, targets or indicators – for example, the proportion of rejects or the time taken to respond to a telephone call – have been established, results can be measured against them. This is a simple method of performance measurement but it can be somewhat crude. It may address only one or two aspects of performance and is not so comprehensive as the use of a battery of statistical control techniques as described below. And, of course, it is only effective if standards are properly set and the information provides a reliable guide to preventive as well as to corrective action.

Inspection

Inspection of the finished product to establish the degree to which it conforms to specification is the traditional method of monitoring quality. But it is severely limited to after-the-event analysis. What it does not do is address the more fundamental aspects of quality – *why* things have gone wrong as well as *what* has gone wrong.

Statistical quality control

Statistical quality control, as described earlier in this chapter, is essentially a preventive measure. It is a before-the-event activity in that unlike inspection it does not wait until the end of the line, when the product has been manufactured or the process completed. Instead, it identifies potential problems before they arise so that preventive rather than corrective actions can be taken.

Statistical process control

Statistical process control techniques detect and help to eliminate unacceptable variations as the process is operating. The statistical part is an analysis of what the process is capable of doing (process capability analysis) in order to establish the criteria by which it will be controlled. The question statistical process control is there to answer is 'What is going wrong with the process?' It assigns causes and points the way to preventive action.

Benchmarking

Benchmarking aims to establish 'best practice' by making inter-firm comparisons. Best practice is expressed in terms of what comparable firms are achieving in the shape of quality standards. Benchmarking is a means of setting standards, but it is also used to monitor company performance against what is being achieved elsewhere. If possible, benchmarking goes beyond simply collecting statistics on what other firms are achieving and tries to find out what methods are being used to get results. Clearly, the full amount of information will be limited or unavailable from some direct competitors and this may reduce the reliability and comprehensiveness of the data. But serious attempts at what is often called 'competitive benchmarking' are well worth making.

Customer service surveys

Surveys can be made of the reactions of customers to the company's products or services. These can take the form of direct enquiries after the event or more regular surveys. The level of customer service in retail organisations can also be monitored by 'mystery shopping' – market research personnel acting as shoppers or telephone enquirers who analyse the service they get (see also Chapter 15).

Internal surveys

Internal surveys can be conducted of the level of service provided by departments to their internal customers within the organisation. Employee-attitude surveys can be used to assess how quality is regarded, and what people are doing about it.

Compare and contrast the various methods of monitoring quality referred to above. Which of these (singly or in combination) do you think would be most relevant in your organisation?

WHO IS RESPONSIBLE FOR ACHIEVING QUALITY?

The simple answer to this question is 'everybody in the organisation', but top management, line management and quality specialists have specific roles.

Top management

Top management set the direction and lead by example. They should ensure that a total quality strategy is developed and communicated to all employees. And they must provide the means for developing, implementing and monitoring the achievement of the strategy. Their role is to ensure that customer care and continual improvement are in the forefront of everyone's minds as they go about their business.

Line managers

Line managers have the prime responsibility for achieving total quality. This is a matter of leadership, communication and involving people in developing and implementing total quality processes and in jointly taking action to improve performance. Line managers are closely involved in continuous improvement. Their role is to monitor quality against standards they have helped to create by using appropriate control techniques and ensuring that action is taken on the basis of the information they provide.

Total quality consultants and specialists

External and internal quality consultants provide advice on approaches to total quality and the particular techniques involved. These may be packaged in the form of a total quality management programme. Consultants may have an important part to play in communicating quality principles and methods, and in training managers and employees in how to apply them. Because quality achievements depend largely on attitudes, their activities can often focus on developing the right approach by organising various kinds of learning experiences.

INVOLVING AND EMPOWERING EMPLOYEES

Total quality will not work unless everyone is involved. This is the main challenge faced by anyone concerned with quality management – 'How can I get people committed to quality?' Clearly, communication and training help, but involvement in the development and application of the principles and practice of total quality achieves a deeper and longer-lasting effect. And empowering people to take control over their own quality practices can be just as important – if not more so.

Involvement

Involvement can be relatively unstructured in the sense that managers and their teams may get together from time to time to identify quality issues and agree methods of dealing with them. More structure can be provided by holding meetings regularly with agendas in the form of progress reports and lists of new issues and action plans.

A fully structured approach can take the form of *quality circles*, which consist of small groups of volunteers who hold regular meetings to discuss and propose ways of improving working methods or arrangements under a trained leader. They ordinarily concentrate on actions that will improve quality but they may extend their remit to cover improvements to productivity or the scope for increasing efficiency or reducing costs. In this extended role they are often called *improvement groups*.

Empowerment

Empowerment is the process of giving people more scope or 'power' to exercise control over, and take responsibility for, their work. It provides greater 'space' for individuals to use their abilities by enabling them and encouraging them to take decisions close to the point of impact.

Empowered decisions are frequently concerned with the achievement of quality in production or service delivery. Empowered employees are encouraged to use their creative and innovative capabilities to identify and address quality problems by themselves and, more frequently, with their fellow team-members. They set quality standards in agreement with their team leaders and monitor their own performance to ensure that these standards are met. They are encouraged to 'manage their own quality' by monitoring their own performance and taking corrective action themselves when a problem arises which is within their own control. When it is caused by a factor they cannot control, they refer the problem to their team leader or a colleague with, ideally, an analysis of the cause of the problem and suggestions on what might be done about it.

Empowerment is not something that happens overnight – it takes time to achieve and requires skilled and sympathetic leadership. Managers and team leaders have to learn how to delegate more and to allow individuals and teams greater scope to plan, act, monitor and review their own performance. But they still have to provide the guidance and support required. And they must in their turn be helped to develop the skills required to function effectively as leaders in an empowered environment.

SUMMARY

- Quality can be defined as the degree of excellence achieved by an organisation in delivering products or services to its customers.

- Quality assurance involves the use of documented procedures designed to ensure that the activities carried out in the organisation result in products or services which meet the requirements and needs of customers.

- Quality control involves the application of data collection and analysis to monitor and measure the extent to which quality assurance requirements have been met in terms of product or service performance and reliability.

- Inspection is an after-the-event activity which is concerned with locating faults when they have already occurred so that they can be put right.

- Statistical quality control uses sampling techniques and mathematical analysis to ensure that during design, manufacturing and servicing, work is carried out and material used within the specified limits required to produce the desired standards of quality, performance and reliability.

- Total quality control processes aim to organise quality into the product or service by pursuing policies of assuring quality and continuous improvement in order to create an environment in which all employees can contribute to improving quality as a normal part of their job.

- Total quality embraces everything an organisation does to deliver value and high levels of satisfaction to its customers. It requires the use of a disciplined, structured and comprehensive approach to quality management. It incorporates quality assurance and quality control techniques but, as the name implies, it includes all aspects of an organisation's activities and concerns everyone in the organisation.

- Total quality management (TQM) can be defined as a systematic way of guaranteeing that all activities within an organisation happen exactly as they have been planned in order to meet the defined needs of customers. It may be regarded as a brand name given to an approach to total quality.

- The major quality standards are ISO 9000 (based on BS 5750) and the EFQM model. But these serve as a framework for designing quality control systems; they are not a substitute for total quality.

- The principles of quality management can be summed up in the words 'customer satisfaction', 'continuous improvement', 'involving everyone', 'creating commitment to quality' and 'looking at the system as a whole'.

- Quality management is a *process,* a way of doing things. It is not a programme with a finite start and finish. The management of quality is a continuous process which may make use of a number of techniques – for example, statistical quality control – but which ultimately depends on the attitudes and behaviour of all concerned. Quality management has to be based on a clearly-stated policy.

- The measurement and monitoring of quality can be achieved by comparison of outputs with standards, inspection, statistical quality control, benchmarking and surveys.

- Total quality will only work if everyone is involved. It is important to empower employees so that they are committed to managing quality themselves.

REFERENCES

1 HUTCHINS D. *Achieve Total Quality.* Hemel Hempstead, Director Books, 1992.
2 DEMING W. E. *Out of the Crisis.* Boston, Mass., MIT Center for Advanced Engineering Study, 1986.
3 COLLARD R. *Total Quality: Success through people* (2nd Edition). London, Institute of Personnel and Development, 1993.
4 JURAN J. M. *Quality Control Handbook.* Maidenhead, McGraw-Hill, 1988.
5 COLLARD, see Note 3 above.
6 CROSBY P. B. *Quality is Free.* New York, McGraw-Hill, 1978.
7 COLLARD, see Note 3 above.

14 Continuous improvement

The philosophy of continuous improvement is that organisations must constantly seek ways of improving their operational systems, the quality of their products and services, and the customer appeal of those products and services. Continuous improvement involves enlisting the ideas and efforts of everyone in the organisation to ensure that a steady stream of suggestions are obtained and acted upon to provide for incremental improvements to operational and quality performance.

'Incremental' is the key word in continuous improvement. It is not about making sudden quantum leaps in response to crisis situations. It *is* about adopting a steady step-by-step approach to improving the ways in which the organisation goes about doing things when carrying out the activities required to deliver value to its customers.

The importance of continuous improvement has been emphasised by Oakland:[1]

> Never-ending or continuous improvement is probably the most powerful concept to guide management. It is a term not well understood in many organisations, although that must begin to change if those organisations are to survive. To maintain a wave of interest in quality, it is necessary to develop generations of managers who not only understand but are dedicated to the pursuit of never-ending improvement in meeting external and internal customer needs.

At the end of this chapter, a reader will understand and be able to explain:

• the significance of continuous improvement

• the process of continuous improvement

• how to assess the impact of continuous improvement teams

• the relevance of the concepts of 'organisational learning' and 'the learning organisation'.

THE SIGNIFICANCE OF CONTINUOUS IMPROVEMENT

In Japan the process of continuous improvement is called *kaizen*, which is a composite of the words *kai* meaning 'change', and *zen* meaning 'good' or 'for the better'. The kaizen management style relies on a foundation of gradual change, building up a culture of quality awareness and constant learning. It is almost the opposite of the Western culture of innovation which is based on sudden change and great leaps forward in business.

The significance of continuous improvement is that it is a day-to-day process in which everyone is involved. As established at Courtelle (the acrylic manufacturers), continuous improvement changes the way people think about their work, and it is the process of change which is important as well as the results achieved. Its significance also rests on the fact that continuous improvement uses the contributions of all employees. It encourages the production of a stream of suggestions for modest, incremental improvements, which can be translated into immediate changes in working practices. As IRS points out:[2] 'Its main focus is customer satisfaction, although resource utilisation is just as important, since it enables an organisation to bring a product or service to a customer at the lowest possible cost.' IRS also states that continuous improvement is based on the belief that it is front-line employees who are best able to come up with the ideas necessary for improvement. Employees must therefore be involved in the process.

THE PROCESS OF CONTINUOUS IMPROVEMENT

Continuous improvement is part of the total quality philosophy but it can exist in its own right as a distinct process. Courtelle, for example, abandoned a formal TQM programme and replaced it with continuous improvement.

The Continuous Improvement Research for Competitive Advantage (CIRCA) unit at Brighton University, as reported by IRS,[3] states that the framework for successful continuous improvement consists of five elements:

1 *Strategy* – Clear strategic goals need to be set for continuous improvement providing 'sign-posted destinations'. These goals should be communicated across the whole organisation and translated into specific targets for teams and individual workers.

2 *Culture* – The culture of the organisation should be developed to support continuous improvement and develop quality awareness. This means defining and communicating values about the need to persist in making incremental improvements to quality as perceived by customers, and about autonomy and empowerment for those involved in improvement on a continuous basis.

3 *Infrastructure* – As recommended by CIRCA, the type of organisation-wide framework necessary for the successful development of continuous improvement includes open management systems, cross-functional management and structures, teamworking, two-way communication processes, joint decision-making, and employee autonomy and participation. This framework depends largely on trust: 'Managers have to trust their workers if they are going to grant them greater responsibility and authority. Empowered employees, similarly, have to trust those in senior positions not to take advantage of employees' ideas to cut jobs. Information is a key component of the creation of greater trust.'

4 *Process* – The processes used in continuous improvement include individual problem-seeking activities, problem-solving groups, suggestion schemes and company-wide campaigns to promote continuous improvement. Continuous improvement does not simply happen by itself. It has to be encouraged and facilitated by management action.

5 *Tools* – Continuous improvement is enhanced by the use of the various problem-solving tools available for individuals and groups. These include Pareto diagrams, cause-and-effect diagrams and various statistical tools such as control charts and scatter diagrams. Benchmarking is another important tool to establish standards for continuous improvement. Groups can use brainstorming techniques to develop ideas.

INTRODUCING CONTINUOUS IMPROVEMENT PROCESSES

The introduction of continuous improvement is by means of communications, involvement, process development and training. Line managers play a key role in all these activities.

Communications

Top management takes the lead by communicating the values governing continuous improvement, emphasising the need for everyone to be involved, and setting out strategic goals. Line managers develop the top management message in association with their teams, translating it into their own departmental context and agreeing team goals.

The communications should emphasise that everyone is expected to operate proactively in the search for improvement rather than let problems arise and then react to them.

Continuous improvement goals may be set as in the examples given below (adapted from *IRS Employment Trends* No. 624, January 1997):

• to meet client needs at a realistic cost

• to ensure the service operates efficiently

• to get things right first time

• to increase customer satisfaction and to improve partnership and teamworking internally

- to achieve the total involvement of the workforce towards continuous improvement
- to become a world-class leader
- to achieve full customer satisfaction
- to improve customer satisfaction and service delivery
- to achieve operational goals as part of the strategic plan
- to continuously improve
- to empower any and every employee to effect change if the result improves customer service
- to improve customer satisfaction while reducing organisational operating costs
- to achieve 800 points on the EFQM model by the year 2000
- to increase awareness and encourage involvement as widely as possible across the Council.

Involvement

The achievement of continuous improvement should involve everyone in the organisation. The IRS survey of continuous improvement policies[4] established that group activities were the most common employee-involvement strategy. Nearly 83 per cent of the organisations had introduced at least one method of involving employees in the continuous improvement process, and of those, 25 per cent had established teamworking or some form of improvement group.

The introduction of continuous improvement requires consideration of how involvement can take place either in the form of group activities or by getting individuals and teams to act as assessors or verifiers. Setting up improvement groups means that an intensive training programme has to be planned and implemented.

Involvement can be organised formally by means of

- *improvement groups* – These act upon broad management-given directives and advice. They are often inter-departmental.

• *problem-solving teams* – These are teams brought together to solve specific management-directed problems.

• *quality circles* – These are teams made up from members of one department or work area, identifying their own projects to develop. They may be composed of volunteers and management. Alternatively, supervision may not be directly involved in the teams' deliberations although they will take part in evaluating proposals and ensuring that they are implemented.

Facilitators may be made available from within the organisation to act as educators, trainers and coaches to teams, not only on specific problem-solving techniques but also on the general philosophy of continuous improvement.

Process development
The development of continuous improvement is partly about creating an infrastructure of involvement processes including suggestion schemes and improvement groups, but it is also concerned with developing appropriate tools and assessment procedures.

As reported in *Management Services* (October 1994), British Gas created a 'Business Improvement Matrix' built round 'enablers' (leadership, policy and strategy, people management, resources and processes) and results (customer satisfaction, people satisfaction, impact on society and business results). The matrix is used by teams to score their achievements against the EFQM categories.

At Courtelle – as reported in *IRS Employment Trends* (March 1991)[5] – the development process emphasised teamworking and included the use of improvement groups which are directly supported by departmental managers. At Lucas Electrical's Cannock factory, as reported in *Works Management* (September 1994), improvement groups became a way of life. They are not voluntary (as was often the case in traditional quality circles).

Employees are told that for one hour a week management wants them to think about nothing but developing improvements.

Developing and training

The purpose of education is to increase awareness of the need for continuous improvement. At Lucas Electrical, awareness and education courses were held to change people's perspective. These consisted of a half-day's appreciation course, a two-day course, and a lot of workshops to get everyone thinking and working in groups. This sort of education aims to change behaviour and by so doing encourage the right sort of attitude to improvement.

Training courses may be held to impart problem-solving and decision-making skills. The use of the various analytical and statistical tools can be demonstrated and practised. At Lucas Electrical the training was extended to the whole workforce and covered quality and maintenance techniques such as failure mode and effects analysis, statistical process control and total productive maintenance (TPM).

The role of line managers

Although continuous improvement involves the whole workforce, line managers still have a key role. Even if self-managed improvement groups or quality circles are in operation, it is up to managers to ensure that ideas are put into practice. Where improvement groups are not voluntary, line managers have an even more important leadership role – one of gaining participation and commitment and providing support, rather than issuing directives. Line managers in an active continuous-improvement environment act as enablers, consultants, facilitators and coaches to individual employees. As the IRS report comments: 'Middle-level managers no longer engage in their traditional performance-monitoring activities but become conduits for training needs and a source of help in implementing suggestions.'

Evaluation

As Dale[6] points out:

> If an improvement process is to progress in a continuous and incremental manner, it is necessary to evaluate it at regular intervals in order to identify the next steps, what else needs to be done, what has worked well and the reasons for this, and what has been unsuccessful; to focus people's efforts, highlight issues and problems and areas of concern or weakness which need to be addressed; and to recognise improvement opportunities.

He suggests that the progress of the improvement process can be measured and demonstrated in terms of

- changes in behaviour and attitude (ie reduced industrial-relations conflicts, or the ease with which procedures crossing a variety of functions are changed)

- improvements in the key operational and business performance indicators (ie reduction in internal defect rates, field failures and warranty claims; increased customer retention and savings from individual improvement projects)

- the degree to which quality improvement projects are aligned with the company's articulated strategies, policies and guidelines.

Holding the gains

Evaluation should lead to action, in Juran's[7] phrase: 'holding the gains'. The gains may include better practices and processes, cost-savings and improved service to customers. Continuous effort is required to ensure that incremental gains are consolidated and become part of normal working practices to the benefit of customers and, therefore, of the organisation.

ORGANISATIONAL LEARNING AND THE LEARNING ORGANISATION

Continuous-improvement organisations are learning organisations. Those concerned with improvement need to know about how organisational learning takes place, about the principle of double-loop learning, and about how learning organisations function and develop.

Organisational learning

Organisations have been described by Harrison[8] as continuous learning systems. Organisational learning can be defined as a process of analysing organisational events, experiences and developments to increase understanding of what needs to be done to improve performance. It is, or should be, happening all the time, and is therefore a means of enhancing continuous improvement.

Organisational learning aims to develop a firm's resource-based capability which, as defined by Harrison, is

> based on what the firm knows and can do, vested primarily in the legacy of knowledge, strategic assets, networks and reputation bestowed by its past human resources, and in the skills, values and performance of its current people.

Argyris[9] makes the point that:

> Learning is not simply having a new insight or a new idea. Learning occurs when we take effective action, when we detect *and* correct error. How do you know when you know something? When you can produce what it is you claim to know.

Single- and double-loop learning

Argyris suggests that learning occurs under two conditions: first, when an organisation achieves what is intended; and second, when a mismatch between intentions and outcomes is identified and corrected. But organisations do not perform the actions that produce the learning – it is individual members of the organisation who behave in ways that produce it, although organisations can create conditions which facilitate such learning.

Argyris distinguishes between single-loop and double-loop learning. Single-loop learning organisations define the 'governing variables' – ie what they expect to achieve in

Figure 11   Single- and double-loop learning

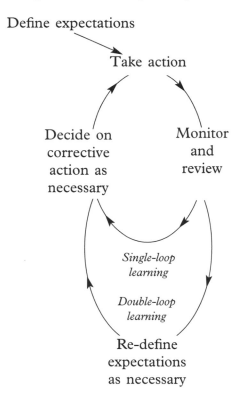

terms of targets and standards. They then monitor and review achievements, and take corrective action as necessary, thus completing the loop. Double-loop learning occurs when the monitoring process initiates action to redefine the 'governing variables' to meet the new situation, which may be imposed by the external environment. The organisation has learned something new about what has to be achieved in the light of changed circumstances and can then decide how this should in turn be achieved. This learning is converted into action. The process is illustrated in Figure 11.

Argyris believes that single-loop learning is appropriate for routine, repetitive issues – 'It helps get the everyday job done.' Double-loop learning is more relevant for complex, non-programmable issues. Double-loop learning questions why the problem occurred in the first place, and tackles its root causes rather than simply addressing its surface symptoms, as happens with single-loop learning. That is why double-loop learning is a necessary part of continuous improvement.

The learning organisation

A 'learning organisation' has been defined by Wick and Leon[10] as one that 'continually improves by rapidly creating and refining the capabilities required for future success'. As suggested by Garvin[11] it is one which is 'skilled at creating, acquiring, and transferring knowledge, and at modifying its behaviour to reflect new knowledge and insights'. He has suggested that learning organisations are good at doing four things:

- *systematic problem solving* which rests heavily on the philosophy and methods of the quality movement. Its underlying ideas include:
  - relying on scientific method, rather than guesswork, for diagnosing problems: what can be described as 'hypothesis-generating, hypothesis-testing' techniques
  - insisting on data rather than assumptions as the background to decision-making: what quality practitioners call 'fact-based management'
  - using simple statistical tools such as histograms, Pareto charts and cause-and-effect diagrams to organise data and draw inferences.

- *experimentation* – This activity involves the systematic search for and testing of new knowledge. Continuous improvement programmes are an important feature in a learning organisation.

- *learning from past experience* – Learning organisations review their successes and failures, assess them systematically and record the lessons learned in a way that employees find open and accessible.

- *transferring knowledge quickly and efficiently throughout the organisation* by seconding people with new expertise, or by education and training programmes, as long as the latter are linked explicitly with implementation.

WHEN CONTINUOUS IMPROVEMENT IS MOST LIKELY TO WORK

The conditions under which continuous improvement is most likely to work well exist when

- top management provides the leadership and direction and ensures that the values underpinning continuous improvement are made clear to all concerned and are acted upon

- middle management supports the philosophy of continuous improvement and is prepared actively to support its introduction and to ensure that effort is sustained

- there is a high-involvement, high-commitment culture in the organisation

- there is trust between management and employees and vice versa. Management must trust employees to act independently, and employees must trust management not to exploit their ideas to their detriment. This trust must be earned. Management must deliver on their promises, and employees – with guidance, encouragement and help – must show that they can be trusted to get on with it

- continuous support is provided by management to the improvement process. This will include facilitating improvement groups and providing the education and training required

- action learning takes place – people learn from the actions they take. This means that processes of evaluation and action planning are required

- double-loop learning takes place

- the organisation functions as a learning organisation

- employees are rewarded for their contributions to

continuous improvement, although such rewards are non-financial and take the form of various kinds of recognition, to teams and individuals, publicly and privately.

What are the most important characteristics of continuous improvement?

What are the three most important things to do when introducing continuous improvement?

The following three criticisms have been made about continuous improvement:

- Appropriating workers' ideas is just another form of managerial control.
- Improvement suggestions make employees party to their own exploitation because this invariably involves harder work.
- A successful suggestion may involve a reduction in the number of jobs.

What replies would you give to these comments?

SUMMARY

- The philosophy of continuous improvement is that organisations must constantly seek ways of improving their operational systems, the quality of their products and services, and the customer appeal of those products and services.

- Continuous improvement involves enlisting the ideas and efforts of everyone in the organisation to ensure that a steady stream of suggestions are obtained and acted upon to provide for incremental improvements to operational and quality performance.

- The significance of continuous improvement is that it is a day-to-day process in which everyone is involved.

- The framework for successful continuous improvement consists of five elements: strategy; culture; infrastructure; processes such as individual problem-seeking activities, problem-solving groups and suggestion schemes; and problem-solving tools.

- The introduction of continuous improvement is by means of communications, involvement, process development and training. Line managers play a key role in these activities.

- The development of continuous improvement is partly about creating an infrastructure of involvement processes including suggestion schemes and improvement groups, but it is also concerned with developing appropriate tools and assessment procedures.

- If an improvement process is to progress in a continuous and incremental manner, it is necessary to evaluate achievements at regular intervals.

- Continuous effort is required to ensure that incremental gains are consolidated and become part of normal working practices to the benefit of customers and, therefore, of the organisation.

- Continuous improvement organisations are learning organisations.

- Continuous improvement is most likely to work well if there is firm top management leadership and direction, support from middle management, a high-involvement, high-commitment culture in the organisation, trust between management and employees and vice versa, and action learning (by which people learn from the actions they take).

REFERENCES

1 OAKLAND J. S. *Total Quality Management.* Oxford, Butterworth-Heinemann, 1989.

2 INDUSTRIAL RELATIONS SERVICES. 'Continuous improvement at Courtelle', *IRS Employment Trends* No. 484, 1991; pp. 11–15.

3 INDUSTRIAL RELATIONS SERVICES. 'Variety through continuous improvement', *IRS Employment Trends* No. 624, 1997; pp. 8–16.

4 IRS, see Note 3 above.

5 IRS, see Note 2 above.

6 DALE B. E. 'Sustaining a process of continuous improvement', *The TQM Magazine*, Vol. 8, No. 2, 1996; pp. 49–51.

7 JURAN J. M. (ed.) *Quality Control Handbook*. Maidenhead, McGraw-Hill, 1988.

8 HARRISON R. *Employee Development* (2nd Edition). London, Institute of Personnel and Development, 1997.

9 ARGYRIS C. *On Organisational Learning*. Cambridge, Mass., Blackwell, 1992.

10 WICK C. W. *and* LEON L. S. 'Creating a learning organisation: from ideas to action', *Human Resource Management*, Summer 1995; pp. 299–311.

11 GARVIN D. A. 'Building a learning organisation', *Harvard Business Review*, July–August 1993; pp. 78–91.

15 Customer care

In profit-making businesses, the achievement of high standards of customer care is generally recognised as an essential element in gaining a competitive edge. In the public and not-for-profit sectors the delivery of satisfactory levels of service to the community in general or to clients and users in particular is one of the key performance indicators.

This chapter explores the processes required by organisations to develop, implement and, importantly, to sustain customer care initiatives. On completing it, a reader will be able to understand and explain:

- the basis and aims of customer care

- how to create a customer care culture

- the meaning of customer service

- the determinants of service quality

- establishing customer expectations

- auditing present customer service arrangements

- setting customer service standards

- measuring and monitoring customer service levels

- developing and implementing customer care strategies and initiatives.

THE BASIS OF CUSTOMER CARE

Customer care is concerned with looking after customers to ensure that their wants, needs and expectations are met or exceeded, thus creating customer satisfaction and loyalty. It is about everything an organisation does when it provides services to its customers. It is also about delighting customers. The aim is not just to meet their needs but to go further – to give them something valuable which they did not expect, and which, perhaps, they did not even know they wanted.

Aims of customer care

The aims of customer care are *1)* to improve customer service by managing all customer contacts to mutual benefit, *2)* to persuade customers to purchase again – not to switch brands or change to another supplier, and *3)* to increase the profitability of a business or the effectiveness of a service-provider organisation.

Ways in which customer care can increase profitability have been listed by Stone[1]:

• less lost business

• fewer lost customers

• repeat sales through increased customer loyalty

• better opportunities for communicating effectively with customers to increase sales

• more scope to identify the potential for increasing revenue from existing customers

• increased revenue and profit by targeting sales to customer needs

• more revenue due to the ability of sales staff to concentrate on calling on higher-revenue prospects

• better and more efficient arrangements for service delivery and therefore lower staff and administration costs.

Why customer care?

It was Jan Carlzon of Scandinavian Airlines System (SAS) who popularised the phrase 'moments of truth', pointing out that whenever customers came into contact with any part of the organisation, the whole was judged by the bit they had seen. Customer care can therefore enhance the organisation's reputation generally.

The need to improve levels of customer care also arises from competitive pressures. Companies compete on the quality of the goods and services they offer, and this extends not only to the products and services themselves but also to the ways in which the service is delivered.

Customer care initiatives can increase profitability, but they can also increase employee motivation and satisfaction by providing them with training to develop their skills and by recognising and rewarding customer care achievements. Research conducted by the Industrial Society[2] showed that

> Managers see a strong, direct link between customer care programmes and financial performance. As well as tangible benefits such as increased business and higher profitability, customer care initiatives are also felt to deliver intangible advantages that include greater staff motivation and better work relationships.

Customer care and total quality

Quality was defined in Chapter 13 as the degree of excellence achieved by an organisation in delivering products or services to its customers. Total quality embraces everything an organisation does to deliver value to those customers. Customer care is therefore an integral part of a total quality initiative, although the pursuit of higher standards of customer care can take place without being associated with formal total quality management processes, especially in service organisations. As Cullen and Hollingworth[3] emphasise: 'A focus on customer satisfaction is the starting point of quality.'

Total quality is concerned with both internal and external customers. The focus of customer care initiatives is usually on external customers but it is also important to pay attention to the levels of service provided internally.

Customer care and competitiveness

Hutchins[4] points out that

> The customer does not know what is technically or organisationally feasible. So the key challenge to a competitive

organisation is to raise the expectations of the marketplace by providing goods and services at quality levels higher than those offered by the competition. As the competition inevitably responds to these challenges, the total quality company will continue to change these expectations, usually in directions not predicted by the competitor.

> Can you think of three reasons why customer care is important?

CREATING A CUSTOMER CARE CULTURE

As the Industrial Society[5] has stated:

> The continuity of customer care depends on establishing a pervasive culture of total customer focus by having continuous customer care conversations through the organisation. All activities must be open to re-examination to identify areas in which customer care can be improved.

The creation of a customer care culture should be based on an understanding of the meaning of customer service, the determinants of service quality, research on customer expectations and an audit of current arrangements. These provide the foundation for the development of customer care strategies and initiatives. Customer care achievements need then to be continually measured and monitored to ensure that the initiatives are working and to provide the basis for remedial action as necessary. The rest of this chapter is devoted to describing each of these activities in turn.

THE MEANING OF CUSTOMER SERVICE

Customer service is to a certain degree intangible because it is about performance – the manner in which the service is delivered – as well as about outcomes – what the customer actually gets. Holberton[6] has offered five different meanings for the term 'customer service':

• the activities involved in ensuring that a product or

service is delivered to the customer on time, in the correct quantities

- the interpersonal working relationships between the staff of a supplier and a customer

- the provision of after-sales repair and maintenance

- the department of an organisation which handles customer complaints

- the order-taking department of an organisation.

DETERMINANTS OF SERVICE QUALITY

Ten determinants of service quality have been identified by Pasuram *et al*:[7]

- *reliability* – consistency of performance and dependability

- *responsiveness* – the willingness or readiness to provide service

- *competence* – having the required skills and knowledge to perform the service

- *access* – approachability and ease of contact

- *courtesy* – politeness, respect, consideration and friendliness of contact personnel

- *communication* – keeping the customers informed in language they can understand, and listening to them

- *credibility* – trustworthiness, believability, honesty

- *security* – freedom from danger, risk or doubt

- *understanding/knowing the customer* – making the effort to understand the customer's needs

- *tangibles* – the physical evidence of service.

DEVELOPING CUSTOMER CARE INITIATIVES

The process of developing customer care initiatives is itemised in the list below.

1 define objectives

2 develop mission and value statements

3 formulate customer care strategy

4 analyse present customer care arrangements

5 assess customer expectations and reactions

6 develop standards and measures

7 measure and benchmark

8 involve staff

9 formulate and implement communication strategy

10 identify and meet training needs

11 implement customer care processes

12 monitor

13 analyse results

14 take action.

The first seven steps have already been covered in earlier sections of this chapter. The others are described below.

ESTABLISHING CUSTOMER EXPECTATIONS

When developing customer care initiatives, it is necessary to establish what the customer expects in terms of 'deliverables': conformity to specifications, quality, price, and reliability in service, in delivery dates, in price and in after-sales service. The two fundamental questions to be answered are: *1)* What services do existing and potential customers want? and *2)* What service is provided by competitors?

Establishing customer expectations can be done by surveying customers. Abbey Life sent out questionnaires to 1,000 clients in each of its business sections. On the credit side, this revealed that customers were satisfied with the time it took for their letters to be answered. But there was dissatisfaction with replies that customers felt did not fully answer their questions. The company now believes it has solved this problem.

Customer expectations can also be assessed by using market research techniques such as opinion surveys and focus groups.

Further information can be obtained from data the organisation may already have in the form of analyses of customer complaints and questions. The opinion of staff about what *their* customers want is worth having. Industry data published by trade associations and in journals is another source.

AUDITING CUSTOMER SERVICE ARRANGEMENTS

It is important to find out what customers want. It is equally important to establish what they get. If the level of service delivery falls below expectations, a customer care gap will be revealed which will need to be filled.

Walker[8] suggests that a customer service audit needs to address both material service and personal service. *Material service* is what is actually delivered. Customers want value for money, products or services which function properly in the way they are supposed to do, efficient delivery systems, and responsive after-sales. *Personal service* can make a greater impact on customer attitudes than material service. Customers want to be dealt with by staff who have the knowledge, skills and competences required. These will include technical and product knowledge, the interpersonal skills needed to handle customers, being able to deal with complaints, and generally being helpful, polite and courteous.

The audit aims to establish what is happening now in order to identify gaps in customer care provision and to indicate what needs to be done to develop customer care strategies, policies and initiatives. The audit is concerned mainly with internal procedures to find out the extent to which they are capable of meeting customer expectations.

However, an analysis of customer expectations carried out by means of questionnaires and market research will provide criteria against which present arrangements can be assessed.

It is at this stage that benchmarking should be carried out to find out, as far as possible, what competitors are doing. This will provide a further check on the extent to which present arrangements are satisfactory, and a basis for developing customer service standards for the organisation.

DEVELOPING A CUSTOMER CARE STRATEGY

Customer care strategies indicate the intentions of the organisation concerning the maintenance and improvement of customer service levels. They emphasise the customer orientation of the business and the part everyone is expected to play. The point may be made in the words of Furnham and Gunter[9] that

> Customer service ... depends crucially on the people who work for the organisation. Good service stems from an organisation's ability, through skilled and knowledgeable staff, to fulfil the obligations it undertakes in its service strategy.

Customer care strategies emanate from top management and set the direction. They may well be summarised in a mission statement such as the Xerox statement reported by Furnham and Gunter:

> Xerox is a quality company. Quality is a basic business principle for Xerox. Quality means providing our external and internal customers with innovation products and services to fully satisfy their requirement. Quality improvement is the job of every Xerox employee.

The mission statement can be supported by value statements which spell out the importance attached to service quality and provide a basis for measuring customer care performance for the organisation, teams and individuals. The statement might refer to such values as

- putting the customer first

- understanding the product or service

- meeting customers' needs and expectations

- the importance of customer care to the organisation.

Mission and value statements underpin the customer care strategy, which will itself reflect the organisation's intentions with regard to

- the analysis of customer expectations and reactions

- setting standards

- measuring and monitoring performance against the standards

- providing staff with information on the importance of customer care (a communication strategy)

- providing leadership to staff

- training staff

- rewarding teams and individuals for good performance

- helping and supporting people to improve performance

- attending to the needs of both internal and external customers

- generally developing a customer care culture which includes managing change, especially the transition from the existing to the desired state.

MEASURING AND MONITORING CUSTOMER SERVICE LEVELS

The measurement of quality service levels is the basis for monitoring and managing customer care. The starting-point is to define standards as described above. The next step is to decide how to measure and monitor the achievement of those standards so that corrective action can be taken. In the formative stages of developing a customer care strategy, measurements indicate where the priorities lie by highlighting areas for concern. The main measurement and monitoring techniques are described below.

Customer questionnaires

Customer questionnaires are probably the most common method of measuring satisfaction. They are presented immediately the given service comes to an end – for example, when leaving a hotel or on completion of a car service. Questionnaires ask customers to rate the service provided from excellent to poor, under such headings as 'politeness/courtesy', 'willingness to help', 'attention to requirements', 'speed of response', 'overall quality'. The responses are analysed and the analysis is fed back to staff. Customer questionnaires provide immediate reactions but they may be completed only by an unrepresentative sample of customers – for example, those who were highly satisfied or dissatisfied.

Customer surveys

Customer surveys, often conducted by market research companies or specialised consumer research firms, cover a much wider and more balanced sample of customers. They ask questions or get customers to respond on a scale (eg 'fully agree', 'generally agree', 'disagree') to such statements as

- Staff respond to customer requests promptly.

- Staff are polite.

- Staff are not always willing to help customers.

- Staff keep their promises to customers.

- Staff do not give you individual attention.

- You have to wait ages to get through to the company by telephone.

- Staff return your calls quickly.

Customer surveys can be comprehensive and illuminating if properly constructed and run. It is best to conduct them regularly in order to analyse trends. Results should be fed back to staff so that action can be taken. But surveys, like questionnaires, cover only shoppers who buy, and they therefore do not identify any aspects of staff behaviour which may cause some shoppers to leave before buying. And customers may find it hard to remember the details of their treatment some time after the event.

An alternative approach which overcomes at least the first of these objections (although it may create other problems) is mystery shopping.

Mystery shopping

Mystery shopping enables the quality of customer service to be assessed at the critical point at which customers come into contact with sales staff – in a retail or service outlet or over the telephone. People (usually from market research firms) are sent into a retail outlet to see how they are treated. Or they may make a telephone enquiry. They then record their observations of how well or badly they were handled against a set of basic standards covering such aspects of service as friendly reception, paying attention to the shopper's wants, helpfulness, knowledge of the product, willingness to listen to and respond to the customer's requests and queries, and avoiding pressurised sales techniques.

At Allied Carpets Group, as reported by IRS,[10] mystery shopping research, together with new technology recording the stores' busiest sales times, was used as a basis for identifying customer needs and restructuring the organisation accordingly. The researchers found that in busy periods there could be long delays before a salesperson approached a customer simply because staff were fully occupied. Allied Carpets dealt with this problem by introducing more flexible staffing arrangements, including raising the proportion of part-time staff.

Mystery shopping could be regarded as a process of spying on staff – catching them unawares and keeping them on their toes by subterfuge rather than effective supervision.

However, specialised mystery shopping consultants claim that the ethics of mystery shopping should be to reward staff for good performance, not to castigate them for poor performance. Those companies which adopt an ethical approach to mystery shopping do not request reports that identify individual staff but rely on general reports setting out strengths and weaknesses in various areas.

Mystery shopping can be extended to call centres and telephone contacts with companies. The same approach is used, but speed of response, helpfulness and understanding are particularly important.

Company analysis

A company can undertake its own analysis of the quality of the service provided to both external and internal customers. At AA Insurance and Abbey Life, equipment has been installed in their telephone call centres which displays the number of calls waiting to be answered. As reported by IDS,[11] Abbey Life also uses its Customer-Focused Quality Initiative to sample and check its employees' work. Errors in policies due to be sent out to clients are analysed and fed back to employees who are given quality targets to attain. Errors are classified as being of presentation, accuracy or completeness. The errors are listed on the employees' own scorecards, at the bottom of which there is space for managers to enter a prescription to rectify any problems.

Some organisations monitor telephone conversations between staff and customers as a basis for feedback.

Benchmarking

Benchmarking – comparing the standards achieved by comparable organisations with those achieved in one's own organisation – is a valuable way of assessing how the organisation is doing.

Supervisors

Supervisors are in the best position to observe from day to day the quality of customer care delivered by their staff. Supervisors should be made aware of the standards they are looking for and they should share this knowledge with their team. In a retail organisation, they can walk around the store and check on how things are going. They can praise good work and discuss how weaknesses can be overcome.

Describe and evaluate the various methods of measuring customer service levels.
Do you think mystery shopping is a legitimate approach to measurement? If so, why? If not, why not?

SETTING CUSTOMER SERVICE STANDARDS

Customer service standards are related to the key aspects of customer service revealed by surveys of customer expectations and present arrangements. The aim is to distil the information to identify critical customer service success factors. These are likely to fall into main categories:

- speed of response and processing of orders, enquiries, complaints, requests for service or spare parts
- quality of response to enquiries or complaints
- backlog of enquiries or complaints
- in call centres, call pick-up and lost-call rate
- number of complaints (as a proportion of total orders)
- time taken between order and delivery
- the extent to which customer expectations have been met in service delivery
- customer reactions to service and perceptions of service quality.

Examples of how qualitative standards might be expressed are:

- response rates – percentage of letters or calls answered in y days

- call pick-up – percentage of calls answered in y seconds or within a certain number of rings (six at Hertz, for example)
- lost-call rates – percentage of inbound calls lost
- backlog – no more than z items to be processed at end of day/week
- field servicing – time to complete service.

More qualitative standards can be developed – for example, on how customers should be approached and be responded to, how complaints should be dealt with, and what information should be provided in response to enquiries. These qualitative standards can be set out under the headings for service quality given earlier in this chapter: 'reliability', 'responsiveness', 'competence', 'access', 'courtesy', 'communication', 'credibility', 'security', 'understanding/knowing the customer' and 'the physical evidence of service'.

Involving staff
Staff should be involved throughout the process. They should certainly participate in developing standards and measures, and should take part in monitoring performance and in deciding on any actions they need to take.

Communications
It is essential to take the trouble to develop and implement a communications strategy. Employees must be informed of the customer care strategies, policies and values of the business. They should be aware of the standards they have to achieve and why they are important – to their own future and security as well as to the prosperity or success of the organisation. They should understand how their performance will be measured and rewarded, and be fully aware of the benefits of the training they will be given in customer care.

Training and education in customer care
Training is the key to successful customer care. The

needs for training are identified by defining the gap between what is being done and what should be being done. The training will be concentrated on the development and practice of interpersonal skills and the provision of information on the organisation's customer care policies and procedures.

Companies, as reported by IDS,[12] place strong emphasis on the importance of including a strong customer care context in induction training. Customer service information is included in training packs at B&Q, Kent's Art and Libraries Department, and Hertz.

Customer service levels need to be continuously improved. All the companies in the IDS survey spent considerable time and resources in reinforcing the importance of the customer to their employees and in developing their skills. For example, London Underground runs a customer training package designed to meet the needs of individual employees. It has rejected the 'sheep-dip' approach by which staff receive the same, and often superficial, training. Instead, the training is composed of six modules, starting with a foundation course and ending with the final and most complex module designed for supervisors only. Other courses, such as training in using public-address equipment, are also provided.

B&Q operates a training course with a strong customer care content. The retail skills framework is a replacement for NVQs, which the company found too time-demanding and bureaucratic. Part of the training known as the product knowledge framework is devoted to increasing employees' knowledge of B&Q's stock. This forms a key part of the company's customer care training.

Going Places runs 45-minute training sessions every Tuesday morning at its shops. Training is designed centrally but is delivered locally by the shops' managers or assistant managers. These managers complete questionnaires, and their comments are used to adjust or refine the training modules.

All employees in Abbey Life's Operations divisions complete a one-day customer care programme called Customers Are Really Essential (CARE). The company also runs courses for team leaders on the 'tools and techniques' of customer service.

NVQs in customer service

National standards for NVQs in customer service have been developed by the Customer Service Lead Body. Staff can be encouraged to take NVQs and given support by their organisations and their managers.

The NVQ units and elements are:

1 *Maintain reliable customer service*
   – maintain records relating to customer service
   – organise own work pattern to respond to the needs of customers
   – make use of networks

2 *Communicate with customers*
   – select information for communication to customer
   – facilitate flow of information between organisation and customer
   – adapt methods of communication to the customer

3 *Develop positive working relationships with customers*
   – respond to the needs and feelings expressed by the customer
   – present positive personal image to customer
   – balance the needs of customer and organisation

4 *Solve problems on behalf of customers*
   – identify and interpret problems facing customers
   – organise solutions on behalf of customers
   – take action to deliver solutions

5 *Initiate and evaluate change to improve service to customers*
   – obtain and use feedback from customer
   – communicate patterns and trends in customer service within the organisation

    – contribute to the evaluation of changes designed to improve service to customers

    – initiate changes in response to customer requirements.

The NVQ units can be used as the framework for ongoing customer care training within the organisation.

Implementation

Implementation involves putting customer care procedures in place and ensuring that they work. It is aided by communication and training, but the main responsibility rests with line management and supervision. Implementation covers such activities as:

- applying turnaround standards for replying to letters

- collecting and analysing samples of work, as at Abbey Life, where records are kept of errors which are fed back to employees who are given quality standards to meet

- installing equipment such as that required to measure performance in call centres which displays the number of calls to be answered or to monitor telephone calls

- developing performance-management processes which involve agreeing targets for customer care performance, reviewing results and preparing personal development plans to improve performance

- regularly holding customer service audits and consumer surveys.

Monitoring, analysing results, taking action

Customer care standards and levels of service have to be continually monitored, and the results analysed and fed back to employees. Feedback has to point the way to specific improvements in the service quality and/or the introduction of new processes to improve service levels, including training.

Assessing team and individual performance

Monitoring and feedback should generate the information required to assess team and individual performance. This should be done systematically and at regular intervals. It should not wait until an annual performance appraisal meeting is held.

Feedback and performance assessments should be constructive. Good performance should be recognised, and areas for further improvement – and how it is to be achieved – agreed.

> In your opinion, what are the three most important things to do when developing customer care initiatives, and why?

SUMMARY

- Customer care is concerned with looking after customers to ensure that their wants, needs and expectations are met or exceeded, thus creating customer satisfaction and loyalty.

- The aims of customer care are *1)* to improve customer service by managing all customer contacts to mutual benefit, *2)* to persuade customers to purchase again – not to switch brands or change to another supplier, and *3)* to increase the profitability of a business or the effectiveness of a service-provider organisation.

- Customer care is an integral part of a total quality initiative, although the pursuit of higher standards of customer care can take place without being associated with formal total quality management processes, especially in service organisations.

- The term 'customer service' can involve delivery, interpersonal relationships, after-sales service, handling complaints and taking orders.

- It is necessary to establish what the customer expects in terms of 'deliverables': conformity to specifications, quality, price, and reliability in service, in delivery dates, in price and in after-sales service.

- It is equally important to establish what customers get. If the level of service delivery falls below expectations, then a customer care gap will be revealed which will need to be filled.

- A customer service audit is required which addresses both material service (what is delivered) and personal service.

- Standards are related to the key aspects of customer service revealed by surveys of customer expectations and present arrangements. The aim is to distil the information to identify critical customer service success factors. These are likely to fall into such categories as speed of response and processing, quality of response, backlogs, complaints, customer reactions.

- The main methods of monitoring levels of service are customer questionnaires, customer surveys, mystery shopping, company analysis, observations by supervisors and benchmarking.

- Customer care strategies reflect the intentions of the organisation concerning the maintenance and improvement of customer service levels. They emphasise the customer orientation of the business and the part everyone is expected to play. Customer care strategies emanate from top management and set the direction. They may well be summarised in a mission statement supported by a statement of core values.

- The key elements in a customer care programme are involving staff, communicating to them, and providing training.

REFERENCES

1 STONE M. 'Evaluating the profitability of customer service' in MARLEY P. (ed.) *The Gower Handbook of Customer Service.* Aldershot, Gower, 1997.

2 INDUSTRIAL SOCIETY *Customer Care.* Managing Best Practice, Issue No. 9. London, The Industrial Society, 1995.

3 CULLEN J. *and* HOLLINGWORTH J. *Implementing Total Quality.* Bedford, JFS Publications, 1982.

4 HUTCHINS D. *Achieve Total Quality.* Hemel Hempstead, Director Books, 1992.

5 INDUSTRIAL SOCIETY, see Note 2 above.

6 HOLBERTON S. 'An idea whose time has not only come but will prevail', *Financial Times,* 30 March, 1991; p. 10.

7 PASURAM A., ZEITHAMI W. *and* BERRY I. 'A conceptual model of service quality and its implications for future research', *Journal of Retailing,* 44, 1985; pp. 12–40.

8 WALKER D. *Customer First: A strategy for quality service.* Aldershot, Gower, 1990.

9 FURNHAM A. *and* GUNTER B. (1993) *Corporate Assessment.* Routledge, London, 1993.

10 INDUSTRIAL RELATIONS SERVICES. 'The customer is boss': matching employee performance to customer service needs'. *IRS Employment Trends* No. 585, June 1995; pp. 7–10.

11 IDS STUDY. *Customer Care.* London, Incomes Data Services, 1992.

12 IDS, see Note 11 above.

16 Change management

Organisations are in a perpetual state of change. This is because of constant external pressures and the need to innovate and adapt to new demands and circumstances. To survive and thrive, businesses have to grow. They must develop new products, expand into new markets, re-organise, re-engineer, introduce new technology and change working methods and practices. Even if this does not happen voluntarily, change may be forced upon them by competition and developments in the business, or by the political and social environment. Managers have to be able to introduce and to manage change, and gain the commitment of their teams to implementing and living with the change.

Change, as Rosabeth Moss Kanter[1] has suggested, can be regarded as the process of 'analysing the past to elicit the present actions required for the future'. It involves moving from a present state, through a transition state, to a future desired state.

On completing this chapter, a reader will:

• understand the change process

• know about the various change management models

• be aware of the various approaches available for managing change.

THE CHANGE PROCESS

The change process starts with an awareness of the need for change to meet internal requirements or to respond to external pressures. An analysis of this situation and the factors that have created it leads to a diagnosis of their distinctive characteristics and an indication of the direction in which action needs to be taken. Possible courses of action can then be identified and evaluated and a choice made of the preferred action.

A decision is then necessary on how to get from here to there. Managing change during this transition state is a critical phase in the change process. It is here that the problems of introducing change emerge and have to be managed. These problems can include resistance to change, low stability, high levels of stress, misdirected energy, conflict, and loss of momentum – hence the need to do everything possible to anticipate reactions and likely impediments to the introduction of change.

The installation stage can also be painful. When planning change there is a tendency for people to think that it will be an entirely logical and linear process of going from A to B. It is not like that at all. As Pettigrew and Whipp[2] describe, the implementation of change is an 'iterative, cumulative and reformulation-in-use process'.

To manage change, it is first necessary to understand the various mechanisms for change as have been expressed in a number of change models that have been summarised below.

CHANGE MODELS

The best-known change models are those developed by Lewin and Beckhard. But other important contributions to an understanding of the mechanisms for change have been made by Thurley, Bandura, and Beer and colleagues.

Lewin

The basic mechanisms for managing change, as described by Lewin,[3] are:

- *Unfreezing* – altering the present stable equilibrium which supports existing behaviours and attitudes: this process must take account of the inherent threats change presents to people and the need to motivate those affected to attain the natural state of equilibrium by accepting change

- *Changing* – developing new responses based on new information

- *Re-freezing* – stabilising the change by introducing the new responses into the personalities of those concerned.

Lewin also suggested a methodology for analysing change which he called 'force-field analysis'. This involves

- analysing the restraining or driving forces which will affect the change: such restraining forces will include the reactions of those who see change as unnecessary or as constituting a threat

- assessing which of the driving or restraining forces are critical

- taking steps both to increase the critical driving forces and to decrease the critical restraining forces.

Beckhard

According to Beckhard,[4] a change programme should incorporate specific processes:

- setting goals and defining the future state or organisational conditions desired after the change

- diagnosing the present condition in relation to these goals

- defining the transition state activities and commitments required to meet the future state

- developing strategies and action plans for managing this transition in the light of an analysis of the factors likely to affect the introduction of change.

Thurley

Thurley[5] described five approaches to managing change:

- *Directive* – the imposition of change in crisis situations or when other methods have failed: this is done by the exercise of managerial power without consultation

- *Bargained* – an approach that recognises that power is

shared between the employer and the employed, and that change requires negotiation, compromise and agreement before being implemented

- *'Hearts and minds'* – an all-embracing thrust to change the attitudes, values and beliefs of the whole workforce: this 'normative' approach (ie one which starts from a definition of what management thinks is right or 'normal') seeks 'commitment' and 'shared vision' but does not necessarily include involvement or participation

- *Analytical* – a theoretical approach to the change process using models of change such as those described above. It proceeds sequentially from the analysis and diagnosis of the situation, through the setting of objectives, the design of the change process, the evaluation of the results, finally to the determination of the objectives for the next stage in the change process. This is the rational and logical approach much favoured by consultants – external and internal. But change seldom proceeds as smoothly as this model would suggest. Emotions, power-politics and external pressures mean that the rational approach, although it might be the right way to start, is difficult to sustain.

- *Action-based* – an approach that recognises that the way managers behave in practice bears little resemblance to the analytical, theoretical model. The distinction between managerial thought and managerial action blurs in practice to the point of invisibility. What managers think is what they do. Real life therefore often results in a 'ready, aim, fire!' outlook on change management. This typical approach to change starts with a broad belief that some sort of problem exists, although it may not be well-defined. The identification of possible solutions, often on a trial-and-error basis, leads to a clarification of the nature of the problem and a shared understanding of a possible optimal solution, or at least a framework within which solutions can be discovered.

From your observations of how change actually takes place in an organisation, which would you say are the most typical approaches to change amongst those listed by Thurley?

Bandura

Ways in which *people* change were described by Bandura:[6]

- People make conscious choices about their behaviours.

- The information people use to make their choices comes from their environment.

- Their choices are based upon the things that are important to them, the views they have about their own abilities to behave in certain ways, and the consequences they think will accrue to whatever behaviour they decide to engage in.

For those concerned in change management, the implications of this theory are that firstly, the tighter the link between a particular behaviour and a particular outcome, the more likely it is that we will engage in that behaviour; secondly, the more desirable the outcome, the more likely it is that we will engage in behaviour that we believe will lead to it; and finally, the more confident we are that we can actually assume a new behaviour, the more likely we are to try it.

To change people's behaviour, we therefore have to change the environment within which they work, convince them that the new behaviour is something they can accomplish (training is important), and persuade them that it will lead to an outcome that they will value. None of these steps is easy.

Beer *et al*

Michael Beer and colleagues[7] suggested that most change programmes are guided by a theory of change that is fundamentally flawed. This theory states that changes in attitudes lead to changes in behaviour. 'According to this model, change is like a conversion experience. Once people "get religion", changes in their behaviour will surely follow.' They believe that this theory gets the change process exactly backwards.

> In fact, individual behaviour is powerfully shaped by the organisational roles people play. The most effective way to change behaviour, therefore, is to put people into a new organisational context, which imposes new roles, responsibilities and relationships on them. This creates a situation that in a sense "forces" new attitudes and behaviour on people.

They prescribe six steps to effective change which concentrate on what they call 'task alignment' – reorganising employees' roles, responsibilities and relationships to solve specific business problems in small units where goals and tasks can be clearly defined. The aim of following the overlapping steps is to build a self-reinforcing cycle of commitment, co-ordination and competence. The steps are:

1 Mobilise commitment to change through the joint analysis of problems.

2 Develop a shared vision of how to organise and manage to achieve goals such as competitiveness.

3 Foster consensus for the new vision, competence to enact it, and cohesion to move it along.

4 Spread revitalisation to all departments without pushing it from the top – don't force the issue: let each department find its own way to the new organisation.

5 Institutionalise revitalisation through formal policies, systems and structures.

6 Monitor and adjust strategies in response to problems in the revitalisation process.

According to Beer and colleagues, this approach is fundamental to the effective management of change. Nonetheless, account should be taken of the likelihood of resistance to change and what can be done about it.

> Beer and colleagues say that you have to 'impose' new roles
> on people to get them to change. What do you think they
> mean by that? Is it a good idea?
> Which of all the above models of change do you think offers
> most insight into the process, and why?

RESISTANCE TO CHANGE

People resist change because it is seen as a threat to
familiar patterns of behaviour as well as to status and
financial rewards. Joan Woodward[8] made this point clearly:

> When we talk about resistance to change we tend to imply
> that management is always rational in changing its direction,
> and that employees are stupid, emotional or irrational in not
> responding in the way they should. But if an individual is
> going to be worse off, explicitly or implicitly, when the
> proposed changes have been made, any resistance is entirely
> rational in terms of his own best interest. The interests of the
> organisation and the individual do not always coincide.

Specifically, the main reasons for resisting change are:

- *the shock of the new* – people are suspicious of anything
  which they perceive will upset their established routines,
  methods of working or conditions of employment – they
  do not want to lose the security of what is familiar to
  them; they may not believe statements by management
  that the change is for their benefit as well as that of the
  organisation – sometimes with good reason; they may
  feel that management has ulterior motives, and
  sometimes the louder are the protestations of
  managements, the less they will be believed

- *economic fears* – loss of money, threats to job security

- *inconvenience* – the change will make life altogether more
  difficult

- *uncertainty* – there is uncertainty about the likely impact
  of the change outside the employment environment

- *symbolic fears* – a small change which may affect some

treasured symbol, such as a separate office or a reserved parking-space, may suggest that bigger changes are on the way, especially when employees are uncertain about how extensive the programme of change will be

- *threat to interpersonal relationships* – anything that disrupts the customary social relationships and standards of the group

- *threat to status or skill* – the change is perceived as reducing the status of individuals or as de-skilling them

- *competence fears* – concern about the ability to cope with new demands or to acquire new skills.

Overcoming resistance to change

Resistance to change can be difficult to overcome even when it is not detrimental to those concerned. But the attempt must be made. The first step is to analyse the potential impact of change by considering how it will affect people in their jobs. The analysis should indicate what aspects of the proposed change may be supported generally or by specified individuals, and which aspects may be resisted. So far as possible, the potentially hostile or negative reactions of people should be identified, taking into account all the possible reasons for resisting change listed above. It is necessary to try to understand the likely feelings and fears of those affected so that unnecessary worries can be relieved and, as far as possible, ambiguities can be resolved. In making this analysis, the individual introducing the change – who is sometimes called the 'change agent' – should recognise that new ideas are likely to be suspect, and should make ample provision for the discussion of reactions to proposals to ensure complete understanding of them.

Involvement in the change process gives people the chance to raise and resolve their concerns and make suggestions about the form of the change and how it should be introduced. The aim is to transfer 'ownership' – a feeling amongst people that the change is something that they are happy to live with because they have been involved in its planning and introduction – it has become *their* change.

Communications about the proposed change should be carefully prepared and worded so that unnecessary fears are allayed. All the available channels as described in Chapter 11 should be used, but face-to-face communications direct from managers to individuals or through a team-briefing system are best.

GUIDELINES FOR CHANGE MANAGEMENT

There are no absolute rules about how to manage change. Clearly, change situations are likely to be unique as far as most of those involved are concerned, and such situations therefore have to be managed in accordance with these special circumstances. But there are certain guidelines which can help in planning and administering the smooth introduction of change. These are:

• The achievement of sustainable change requires strong commitment and visionary leadership from the top.

• Understanding of the culture of the organisation, and of the levers for change which are most likely to be effective in that culture, is vital.

• Those concerned with managing change at all levels should have the temperament and leadership skills appropriate to the circumstances of the organisation and its change strategies.

• It is important to build a working environment which is conducive to change. This means developing the firm as a 'learning organisation'.

• Although there may be an overall strategy for change, it is best tackled incrementally (except in crisis conditions). The change programme should be broken down into actionable segments for which people can be held accountable.

• People support what they help to create. Commitment to change is improved if those affected by change are allowed to participate as fully as possible in planning and implementing it. The aim should be to get them to 'own' the change as something they want and will be glad to live with.

- The reward system should encourage innovation and recognise success in achieving change.

- Change implies streams of activity across time and 'may require the enduring of abortive efforts or the build-up of slow incremental phases of adjustment which then allow short bursts of incremental action to take place' – Pettigrew and Whipp[9].

- Change will always involve failure as well as success. The failures must be expected and learned from.

- Hard evidence and data on the need for change are the most powerful tools for its achievement, but establishing the need for change is easier than deciding how to satisfy it.

- It is easier to change behaviour by changing processes, structure and systems than to change attitudes or the corporate culture.

- There are always people in organisations who can act as champions of change. They will welcome the challenges and opportunities that change can provide. They are the ones to be chosen as change agents.

- Inept management of change will guarantee that change will be resisted.

- Every effort must be made to protect the interests of those affected by change.

GAINING COMMITMENT TO CHANGE

These guidelines point in a single direction: once it is decided why changes are necessary, what the goals are and how they are to be achieved, the most important task is to gain the commitment of all concerned to the proposed change.

A strategy for gaining commitment to change should cover five phases:

1 *Preparation* – In this phase, the person or persons likely to be affected by the proposed change are contacted in order to be made aware of the fact that a change is being contemplated.

2 *Acceptance* – In the second phase, employees are consulted on the contemplated change. They are provided with information on the purpose of the change, and are asked for their opinion on the form it should take and how it might be implemented. The effect it will have on those concerned is discussed. The aim is to achieve understanding of what the change means and to obtain a positive reaction. This is more likely if
   – the change is perceived to be consistent with the mission and values of the organisation
   – the change is not thought to be threatening
   – the change seems likely to meet the needs of those concerned
   – there is a compelling and fully understood reason for change
   – those concerned are involved in planning and implementing the change programme
   – it is understood that steps will be taken to mitigate any detrimental effects of the change.

It may be difficult, even impossible to meet all these requirements. That is why the problems of gaining commitment to change should not be under-estimated. During this phase, the extent to which reactions are positive or negative can be noted and action taken accordingly. It is at this stage that original plans may have to be modified to cater for legitimate reservations or second thoughts. There is no point in consultation unless the views expressed are listened to and, as far as possible, acted upon. (If they are not accepted, the reasons why should be explained.)

3 *Managing the transition* – During the third phase, the change is implemented. This is the transitional stage and it has to be managed carefully. The change process and people's reaction to it need to be monitored. There

will inevitably be delays, setbacks, unforeseen problems and negative reactions from those faced with the reality of change. A response to these reactions is essential so that corrective action can be taken, and valid criticisms can be acted upon or explanations given of why it is believed that the change should proceed as planned.

4 *Implementation* – When implementing change the aim is to get it accepted so that, in use, its worth becomes evident. The decision is made at this stage on whether to continue with the change or whether it needs to be modified or even aborted. Account should again be taken of the views of those involved.

5 *Institutionalising change* – Finally, and after further modifications as required, the change is institutionalised and becomes an inherent part of the organisation's culture and operations.

SUMMARY

- The change process starts with an awareness of the need for change to meet internal needs or to respond to external pressures. This is followed by an analysis and diagnosis of the situation, and the identification and evaluation of possible courses of action, leading to a decision. It is then necessary to manage the transition between the present state and the desired future state. Finally, the change is installed, which can be a painful process.

- There are various models of how change takes place, each of which provides some insight into this complex process. The main models are those developed by Lewin, Beckhard, Thurley, Bandura, and Beer and colleagues.

- People resist change because they are suspicious of anything that will upset their routines and possibly make their life more difficult. They may fear loss of money or believe that the change threatens their job security. They may dislike the uncertainty, inconvenience or disruption to personal relationships which they fear from the change. They may worry about loss of status and being unable to cope with new demands.

- Resistance to change may be difficult, sometimes impossible, to overcome. But the attempt should be made by analysing possible reactions and by involving people in planning and implementing change. And good communications help.

- There are no absolute rules about how to manage change. Clearly, change situations are likely to be unique as far as most of those involved are concerned, and such situations therefore have to be managed in accordance with those special circumstances. But there are certain guidelines as set out earlier in this chapter which can help in planning and administering the smooth introduction of change.

- The most important task is to gain the commitment of all concerned to the proposed change. This can be achieved by preparing for change thoroughly, gaining understanding and acceptance of the reasons for change, managing the transition carefully, and implementing the change in a way which ensures, as far as possible, that it is accepted so that, in use, its worth becomes evident.

REFERENCES

1 KANTER R. M. *The Change Masters*. London, Allen & Unwin, 1984.

2 PETTIGREW A. and WHIPP R. *Managing Change for Competitive Success*. Oxford, Blackwell, 1991.

3 LEWIN K. *Field Theory in Social Science*. New York, Harper & Row, 1951.

4 BECKHARD R. *Organisation Development: Strategy and Models*. Reading, Mass, Addison-Wesley, 1969.

5 THURLEY K. *Supervision: A Reappraisal*. London, Heinemann, 1979.

6 BANDURA A. *Social Boundaries of Thought and Action*. Englewood Cliffs, NJ., Prentice Hall, 1986.

7 BEER M., EISENSTAT R. and SPECTOR B. 'Why change programs

don't produce change', *Harvard Business Review.* November-December, pp. 158–166, 1990.

8 WOODWARD J. 'Resistance to change', *Management Review,* vol. 8, 1968.

9 PETTIGREW *and* WHIPP, see Note 2 above.

Glossary of management terms

Accountability Having to account for one's actions and results to a higher authority.

Activity What people do.

Allocating work Assigning tasks to a person or a group of people in order to achieve a purpose.

Authority The process of exerting influence on others in order to get things done.

> **Authority to act** The right to make certain decisions or to act in particular ways within defined limits or constraints.

> **Authority to authorise** Confirming or agreeing that people can take certain actions.

> **Authority to command** Giving people instructions or orders.

Benchmarking Establishing 'best practice' by making inter-firm comparisons. Best practice is expressed in terms of what comparable firms are achieving in areas such as quality standards or levels of productivity. Benchmarking is a means of setting standards, but it is also used to monitor company performance against what is being achieved elsewhere.

Commitment Belief in and acceptance of the organisation and its goals, and willingness to make efforts on behalf of the organisation.

Committees Formally-constituted bodies of people who meet regularly to discuss policy and planning issues, review performance and agree on actions in accordance with terms of reference.

Competences The things people need to be able to

understand and do in order to perform effectively. They provide the basis for National Vocational Qualifications and professional standards such as those produced by the Institute of Personnel and Development and the Management Charter Institute.

Competencies The behaviours that produce effective performance.

> **Competency framework** A schedule of generic competencies – ie those competencies that are applicable throughout the organisation.

> **Competency profile** The competencies that are applicable to a generic role (eg sales staff) or a particular role (eg a sales manager).

Continuous improvement The process of ensuring that organisations constantly seek ways of improving their operational systems, the quality of their products and services, and the customer appeal of those products and services.

Controlling Monitoring and measuring performance, comparing results with plans, and taking corrective action when required.

Co-ordination Ensuring that people work well together to achieve a common purpose through unified effort.

Core values Express beliefs in what is best or good for the organisation and what sort of behaviour is desirable.

Critical success factor For individuals or teams, a feature of the work (or aspects of performance) vital to the achievement of objectives. For the organisation, any one of the drivers which are vital to the achievement of corporate goals.

Customer care Looking after customers to ensure that their wants, needs and expectations are met or exceeded, thus creating customer satisfaction and loyalty.

Customer-focused organisation An organisation

which strongly emphasises the need for excellence in customer care.

Customer service The activities involved in ensuring that a product or service is delivered to the customer on time, in the correct quantities. The maintenance of good interpersonal working relationships between the staff of a supplier and a customer. The provision of good after-sales maintenance and repair.

Delegation The commitment of authority or power to someone. Delegation involves managers' giving people the authority to do something rather than carrying it out themselves.

Direction The planning, use and control of resources to achieve a result.

Distribution The storage of finished goods and their efficient delivery to wholesalers and retailers or direct to customers.

Duty The responsibility for carrying out an activity or task.

Feedback The process of providing information on what has been done in order to take further action where necessary.

Financial accounting Recording the revenue received and the expenditure incurred by a company so that its overall performance over a period of time and its financial position at a point in time can be ascertained.

Financial management The management of all aspects of the financial affairs of an organisation: financial planning, financial accounting (keeping the books and preparing financial reports and statements), management accounting (measuring and analysing financial performance) and managing cash flows.

Function, organisational Part of an organisation in which various related activities or tasks are carried out to achieve a desired result that is contributory to the organisation's overall output.

Goal The result the organisation or individual wants or is expected to achieve.

High-involvement organisations Organisations in which management puts into effect involvement programmes which genuinely provide for employees to take part in decision-making processes on matters that affect them.

High-performance organisations Organisations in which the focus is on achieving and sustaining high levels of performance in terms of profitability, output, productivity, innovation and quality – this could be expressed in terms of continuous improvement policies and processes.

Human resource management (HRM) Term often used as a modern alternative for 'personnel management'. HRM focuses on the development of integrated HR strategies and a cohesive set of processes for managing, developing and rewarding people.

Inventory control Ensuring that the optimum amount of inventory or stock is held by a company so that its internal and external demand requirements are met economically.

IT (information technology) management Developing and operating systems for collecting, storing, processing and communicating information. This includes the specification and selection of hardware, the design of networks and the specification or development of software applications.

Job design The process of deciding on the content of a job or role in terms of its duties and responsibilities, the methods used to carry out the work, and the relationships existing between the job-holder and others.

Key result area Part of a job which makes a particularly significant contribution to the achievement of its overall purpose and for which objectives can be set.

Learning organisation An organisation that

'continually improves by rapidly creating and refining the capabilities required for future success' (Wick and Leon, see Chapter 14, Note 10).

Line managers Managers who are responsible for a mainstream activity which directly impacts on the results achieved by an organisation.

Line of command The line of authority which descends through an organisational hierarchy.

Management Deciding what to do and getting it done through and with other people by making the best use of the available resources.

Management accounting Providing information to management on present and projected costs and on the profitability of individual projects, products, activities or departments as a guide to decision-making and financial planning.

Management style The approach a manager uses in leading his or her team and exercising authority.

Management techniques Systematic and analytical methods such as production control, marketing research, cost-volume-profit analysis, job evaluation and operational research, which are used by managers to assist in decision-making, planning and control.

Manager A person who is responsible for the operation of a discrete organisational unit or function and who has authority over other people working in that unit or function.

Marketing The management process responsible for identifying, anticipating and satisfying customer requirements profitably.

Meetings Gatherings of people in order to discuss particular issues and reach a collective decision.

Mission statement An indication in broad terms of why the organisation exists, what it is there to do and how it intends to do it.

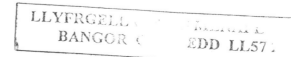

Monitoring   Measuring and observing what is happening as it happens so that swift action can be taken as required.

Motivating   Enthusing people into action so that they work to the best of their ability to achieve the required results as part of a team.

Norms   The unwritten rules of behaviour.

Objective   A broad definition of what the business or individual is expected to achieve on a continuing and progressive basis.

Operational managers   Managers who are responsible for a major function, such as production or distribution, which directly impacts on organisational results.

Operations management   The planning, direction and control of the fundamental activities which the organisation exists to carry out. These activities are to make, provide or sell products or services.

Organisation   The design, development and maintenance of a system of co-ordinated activities in which individuals and groups of people work co-operatively under authority and leadership towards commonly understood and accepted goals.

Organisation behaviour   The way in which people act in the organisation individually or in groups.

Organisation climate   The working atmosphere of an organisation, as perceived by its members.

Organisation design   The process of analysing and determining roles and relationships in an enterprise so that collective effort is explicitly organised to achieve specific ends.

Organisation development   Improving the overall effectiveness of the organisation by integrating activities, team-building, developing a more positive culture and handling inter-group relations.

Organisation structures   The framework for getting work done. The structures define and clarify how the activities required are grouped together into units, functions and departments, who is responsible for what, who reports to whom, and the lines of authority that emanate from the top of the organisation.

Organisational (or corporate) culture   The pattern of values, norms, beliefs, attitudes and assumptions which may or may not have been articulated but which shape the ways in which people behave and things get done.

Organisational learning   A process of analysing organisational events, experiences and developments to increase understanding of what needs to be done to improve performance.

Organising   Deciding who does what and defining roles and relationships within the organisation or unit.

Performance   Carrying into effect policies, programmes and plans in order to achieve defined and measurable objectives, and the results of doing so.

   Performance management   Increasing organisational effectiveness by improving the performance of managers and staff as individuals or teams.

   Performance measures   Methods of expressing in quantified terms how well the individual or team has performed in carrying out the allocated tasks and in achieving targets and standards.

Personnel management   The management and development of people in ways that contribute to the achievement of organisational effectiveness and that simultaneously meet their own needs for a satisfactory quality of working life, for security, and for the opportunity to use their abilities and develop their experience and skills. The terms 'personnel management', 'personnel development' and 'human resource management' are often used interchangeably.

Planning   The process of deciding on a course of action, ensuring that the resources required to implement the action will be available, and scheduling the programme of work required to achieve a defined end-result.

Policy A statement of principles or common purposes which serves as a continuing guideline and establishes limits for discretionary action by management.

Politics In organisations, a common understanding of who has the decision-making power and how decisions are made, so that influence – which often has hidden aspects – can be exerted without going through normal channels.

Power The capacity to impress the dominance of one's goals or values on others.

Prioritisation Deciding on the relative importance of each of a range of demands or tasks so that the order in which they are undertaken can be determined.

Procedure A method or system for getting something done.

Procedure planning Deciding how the work will be carried out.

Production The procurement, deployment and use of resources to manufacture products for distribution and sale to customers. It transforms inputs, in the shape of raw materials and bought-in or subcontracted parts, into outputs in the form of finished goods.

Production management Planning and controlling the use of people, materials, plant and machines to attain the company's objectives for output, and the achievement of manufacturing programmes, quality and productivity.

Purchasing management Also known as supplies management, procurement or buying, the acquisition in the right quantities and at the right price of the materials, plant, equipment and bought-in parts or assemblies required by the organisation.

Quality The degree of excellence achieved by an

organisation in delivering products or services to its customers.

Quality assurance The use of documented procedures designed to ensure that the activities carried out in the organisation (design, development, manufacturing, service delivery) result in products or services which meet the requirements and needs of customers. The underpinning philosophy of quality assurance is that right methods will produce right results (quality products or services).

Quality control Monitoring and measuring the extent to which quality assurance requirements have been met in terms of product or service performance and reliability.

Research and development The design and development of new products or the modification of existing products in order to create or satisfy customer needs and wants, now and in the future.

Resourcing Deciding how many and what sort of people will be required, and when. Assessing demands for finance, facilities, materials and bought-in parts in terms of amounts, types and when they need to be available.

Responsibility The taking on of particular obligations for performing a job or a task and achieving the required results. Job-holders are in a position of responsibility if they are liable to be called to account for what they do.

Role The part a person plays in fulfilling his or her responsibilities.

Scheduling Determining the sequence and timescales of the operations and events required to produce results within a deadline.

Selling The process of persuading customers to buy and continue to buy the products or services of the business.

Service-oriented organisations Organisations in which

the focus is on service delivery and improving levels of service to customers or clients.

Staff departments   Departments of which the function is to support and provide services to line departments.

Standard of performance   The level of attainment expected of job-holders defined in terms of the observable behaviour that will indicate the extent to which the job or task has been well done.

Statistical process control   A technique for detecting and helping to eliminate unacceptable variations as a process is operating.

Statistical quality control   The use of sampling techniques and mathematical analysis to ensure that during design, manufacturing and servicing, work is carried out and material used within the specified limits required to produce the desired standards of quality, performance and reliability.

Strategic management   A continuing process consisting of a sequence of activities: strategy formulation, strategic planning, implementation, review, and updating. It requires general management to look ahead to what they want the organisation to achieve in the middle or relatively distant future.

Strategy   A broad statement of intent outlining where the organisation as a whole (or where a significant part of it) is going in the longer term to achieve its objectives.

Success criteria   The factors which will be used to measure the organisational results obtained.

Supplies   All the materials, plant, equipment and bought-in parts or job-assemblies required by the company as inputs from which to derive outputs.

Target   A specified result to be attained which will be described in quantitative terms.

Task   What a person or a group is expected to do in a specific activity area.

Team A small number of people with complementary skills who 'are committed to a common purpose, performance goals and approach for which they hold themselves mutually accountable' (Katzenbach and Smith, see Chapter 5, Note 2).

Total quality An overarching concept which embraces everything an organisation does to deliver value and high levels of satisfaction to its customers. Total quality implies the use of a disciplined, structured and all-embracing approach to quality management. It incorporates quality assurance and quality control techniques but, as the name implies, it includes all aspects of an organisation's activities and concerns everyone in the organisation. It is thus focused on delivering quality services to internal as well as external customers.

Total quality control The organisation of quality into the product or service by pursuing comprehensive policies of assuring and controlling quality.

Total quality management An approach to guaranteeing that all activities within an organisation happen in the way they have been planned in order to meet the defined needs of customers. It may be regarded as a method of systematising or packaging the notion of total quality so that it can act as a brand-name which managements can identify with when introducing quality programmes.

Values The basic beliefs about what is good or best for the organisation, about what management thinks is important, and about what should or should not happen.

Value-driven When the *value set* (see below) of an organisation is shared and acted upon throughout the business.

Value set/system The core values (*qv*) adopted by an organisation.

Working-parties Groups of people who are brought

together to get something done – to deal with a problem, to discuss and plan an innovation or to prepare for and oversee a project. They may also be called project teams or task forces.

Professional standards index

This index cross-references to pages in the text the main subject areas as set out in the Professional Standards of the Institute of Personnel and Development for *Managing Activities.*

THE NATURE OF MANAGERIAL WORK

QUALITY AND CONTINUOUS IMPROVEMENT

Index

The People and Organisations series and Core Management studies

The only route to a professional career in personnel and development is through the achievement of the IPD's professional standards. One of the three fields that make up these standards, the new Core Management standards define the essentials for competently managing and developing people. They are compatible with an N/SVQ at Level 4 in management.

IPD Publications has five new books in the *People and Organisations* series as textbooks for the new Core Management standards. The texts of these five books and their titles will closely follow the Core Management syllabus. The titles of the books are:

Managing Activities	Michael Armstrong
Managing Financial Information	David Davies
Managing in a Business Context	David Farnham
Managing Information and Statistics	Roland and Frances Bee
Managing People	Jane Weightman

Managing Financial
Information
David Davies

Managing Financial Information is a practical explanation of the interface between the finance and HR functions in organisations. It analyses thoroughly many areas that managers may find daunting, and includes test questions and work-based exercises to assist competent learning.

It examines:

- balance sheets
- trading and profit and loss accounts
- budgeting
- costing.

David Davies is a principal lecturer in financial management at the University of Portsmouth. A qualified accountant with a Masters degree in management from Henley Management College, he previously spent 17 years in the private and public sectors. He currently lectures on post- and undergraduate courses, as well as undertaking consultancy work.

June 1999
£13.95
0 85292 782 7
Paperback
240 pages approx.
246 × 177mm format

Managing in a Business Context
by David Farnham

Managing in a Business Context illustrates the framework in which businesses are working in Britain today. Beginning with the nature of strategy and how strategy can be converted into practice, it then considers the issues of wider concern to HR practitioners and business managers in general.

It examines:

- economics, politics and political systems, and their effect on the workplace
- social and legal structures, and how they impinge on the private and public sectors
- the technological revolution and its effect on working practices
- business ethics and the impact of an international climate.

Professor David Farnham holds the chair in Employment Relations at the University of Portsmouth. He has also written *Employee Relations in Context*, published by the IPD.

July 1999
£15.95
0 85292 783 5
Paperback
256 pages approx.
246 × 177mm format

Managing Information and Statistics
Roland and Frances Bee

Managing Information and Statistics is a hands-on guide that explains how the apparently esoteric discipline of statistics can be an invaluable management tool. Tables, diagrams and graphs are explained in detail; surveys, forecasting and the principles of relationships between data each have their own sections.

It examines:

- how to produce reports and presentations to the highest standard
- how to use general statistical packages
- how to apply statistical thinking to people-management issues
- how to manage data effectively.

Frances and Roland Bee are experienced training consultants and have written three other highly successful IPD books – *Training Needs Analysis and Evaluation, Constructive Feedback, Customer Care* and *Project Management.*

June 1999
£14.95
0 85292 785 1
Paperback
384 pages approx.
246 × 177mm format

Managing People
by Jane Weightman

Managing People is an approachable introduction to working with people and to understanding how people work. It discusses the psychology of the workplace, including its fundamental characteristics, differences between individuals, and how people learn. *Managing People* also studies issues of central concern to all managers, such as performance management, and training and development.

It examines:

- how to motivate your employees
- differing work patterns and their implications for the workplace
- how to manage work-related stress.

Jane Weightman is a psychologist and has been associated with UMIST since 1980. She has carried out research into a wide range of management-related topics and has written widely in a range of journals. Her books include *Competencies in Action* and *Managing People in the Health Service*, both published by the IPD.

May 1999
£15.95
0 85292 784 3
Paperback
240 pages
246 × 177mm format